Comic Strip Characters Celebrate 100 Years!

The Magazine For Doll Lovers

DollWorld®

August 1996

Disney Dolls
Dynamite Collectibles

Discover
State Fair Dolls

Charles Ventura
Paper Doll Artistry

Girl of the Limberlost
Complete Pattern for
Cloth Doll and Costume

America's
Doll Museums
Part 3

Mary Poppins

Make Your Own Doll Greeting

Doll World®

AUGUST 1996 • VOLUME 20 • NUMBER 4

64

34

10

July and August are prime vacation months. Some of us are heading to the beach, others to the mountains and still others to the woods. Some of us think city sights are tops and others combine as many of the above as possible. With the electronic world linking us together in ever-tighter "webs," we're often only a few punched-in numbers away from the office. In fact, television commercials would lead us to believe we ought to *want* to send a fax from the beach.

Personally, I don't want to be accessible on the beach. I intend to spend a quiet week in the North Woods. I hope to hear the loons, do some cross-stitch, write a few letters and read as many books as I possibly can. Spending some quiet time with my husband sounds pretty good too, and perhaps we'll catch a few walleyes and northerns.

Whether you spend your vacation even more engrossed than ever or take the time to get away from the electronic world, I hope you have a good one. All of us deserve a break. We'll be ready for the rest of the year.

Cary Raesner

Letters From Our Readers

Holly Hobbie

It's true Holly Hobbie has been around for a very long time. She goes well with a country home. I have quite a few Holly Hobbie collectibles.

I've enclosed pictures of my porcelain musical doll and stuffed soft dolls. I would love to see a new interest in Holly Hobbie—she is an American tradition like Raggedy Ann.

Joyce A. Smyth, Atwater, Calif.

Francie

I enjoy your magazine, as I feel the articles are written by collectors for collectors. However, in "Modern Dolls & Their Carrying Cases" by Cindy Sabulis (*Doll World*, February 1996), I feel there is an error.

On page 35, there appears to be a Francie head on a Barbie doll body. Francie's body has a smaller bust and almost flat feet. Francie is also shorter than Barbie.

Alice Hasenbank, Kansas City, Kan.

Doll World®

Editorial Director	Vivian Rothe
Editorial Coordinator	Vicki Steensma
Editor	Cary Raesner
Copy Editors	Cathy Reef Läna Schurb
Production Manager	Vicki Macy
Creative Coordinator	Shaun Venish
Production Artist	Sandra Bauman
Production Coordinator	Sandra Beres
Production Assistants	Carol Dailey Cheryl Lynch Darren Powell
Photography	Tammy Christian Nora Elsesser
Photography Assistant	Linda Quinlan

Publishers	Carl H. Muselman Arthur K. Muselman
Chief Executive Officer	John Robinson
Marketing Director	Scott Moss
Newsstand Consultant	Angelo Gandino

KNAPP & ASSOCIATES, INC.
Advertising Representative
Home Office
2112 Riverview Ave., Kansas City, KS 66102
(913) 371–8286, Fax (913) 371–8290

President: Everett G. Knapp III
(913) 371–8288

Vice President
Director of East & West Coast Offices
Tamara Hanes
(913) 371–8287

New Business Manager: Barbara Pitts
(913) 371–8288

Direct Response Marketing: Marilyn Kelly

PR/Marketing/Advertising
Services Manager: Laura Bollin
(913) 371–8289

Central Advertising Manager: Jack Kelly

Midwest Sales Manager: Terry L. Tessier

European Representative: Jim Young

Canadian Representative: Jim Clarke
(800) 571–2284

Classified Advertising: Sharyl Berry
306 East Parr Road, Berne, IN 46711
(219) 589–8741

DOLL WORLD (ISSN 1066-4726, USPS 502-810) is published bimonthly by House of White Birches, 306 East Parr Road, Berne, IN 46711, (219) 589–8741, Fax (219) 589–8093. Second-class postage paid at Berne, IN 46711, and additional mailing offices. Canada Post International Publications Mail Product (Canadian Distribution) Sales Agreement No. 0253898. Copyright © 1996 House of White Birches.

SUBSCRIPTIONS: $17.77 per year in USA, CAN $26.95 in Canada. Please send all subscription-related correspondence to *Doll World*, P.O. Box 9002, Big Sandy, TX 75755, or call (800) 829–5865. To change your address, send your current mailing label along with your new address as soon as possible. Allow six weeks for address changes.

NEWSSTAND DISTRIBUTION: For Retail Display Allowance information, contact Kable News Co., 641 Lexington Ave., New York, NY 10022, (212) 705–4600.

RETAILERS: If you are not presently being provided copies of this magazine by your area newsstand wholesaler, contact The Needlecraft Shop to set up a direct account: (903) 636–4011.

CONTRIBUTORS: Please send all manuscripts to *Doll World*, 306 East Parr Road, Berne, IN 46711. Publisher assumes no responsibility for return or safety of unsolicited materials. Every effort is made to return submissions if accompanied by return postage. Responsibility for advertised products lies with the advertisers. *Doll World* will not knowingly publish fraudulent materials and is not liable for any damages arising from the purchase or use of any products. If you have any consumer complaints concerning goods purchased from our advertisers, please send us written notification to aid our screening process.

POSTMASTER: Send change of address to *Doll World*, P.O. Box 9002, Big Sandy, TX 75755.
Printed in USA. GST Account Number 135414274.

Georgetown Collection
Artist's Edition®

Shown smaller than actual size of 11" seated (18" head to toe). Plush teddy bear included.

"I want my Mommy!"

Nicole has been very good for Grandma — almost the whole afternoon. But after a while, there comes a time when a little girl just wants to go home. Biting her lip…hugging her Teddy…she bravely manages not to cry. And everyone's happy to hear Mommy's footsteps coming up the walk.

Don't make her wait any longer. Give your heart to *Nicole* today. After all — she just wants to go home — with you!

Nicole is an *Artist's Edition*® available exclusively from the Georgetown Collection.

Disney Doll Celebrities

By Carolyn Mingus

"No one can truly say how many dolls have evolved from the characters created by Walt Disney. Since the 1930s, one after another of his little creatures have attained doll status, and the parade continues to grow."

—20th Century Dolls *by Johana Gast Anderton*
(Wallace-Homestead Book Co.)

Madame Alexander 8" doll in Round-Up Days outfit from the Mickey Mouse Club of the 1950s. Sold at Disneyana convention.

As a child, John Anderson delighted in a bisque set of Snow White and the Seven Dwarfs kept in his grandparents' corner cabinet. As an adult, Anderson's interest has become a passion for collecting the best of Disney memorabilia—including dolls that represent Disney characters produced over the last 60 years.

A Collection Begins

John's wife, Yvonne, shares his appreciation of the Disney world and has worked enthusiastically at their Disney-related activities over the years. The couple recognize the beauty of Disney dolls and collectibles as "good" art, and as a reflection of the culture that created it. In fact, when John and Yvonne were asked what they'd save first if their house caught fire, they answered without a moment's hesitation, "Our 1935 Mickey Mouse character doll" (see page 7).

The Andersons began their personal collection in a small way in the late 1960s. At the time, not many Disney pieces were to be found at the malls. Intrigued by Disneyana, John and Yvonne attended all the local antique shows, sought out Disney items, advertised their interest in the *Antique Trader*, and soon became known for their personal collection.

The Andersons' interest in the area was further heightened when they visited Disneyland with their children in 1970 and then attended a three-day convention of the national Mickey Mouse Club with some 150 other Disney fans. Today, their Disney stories and Disney friends are legion.

Good Friends

The Andersons' journey with Disneyana has been filled with smiles and many good friends—artists who drew the early Disney creations, the people whose voices we identify as Disney characters, participants in the national and Colorado wings of the

Come down for the most magical Teddy Bear and Doll Convention of all!

It's November 14 - 17, during the 25th anniversary celebration of Walt Disney World!

The ninth annual Walt Disney World get-together promises to be the biggest and best ever, complete with extraordinary first-time unveilings, spectacular limited-edition collectibles created just for this show, and appearances by an incredible number (60 at last count) of the world's top doll and teddy bear artists. All in the magical, memorable setting of Disney's 25th anniversary celebration.

Wrap Up a Package Now

You don't want to miss a minute of the fun, and you won't with one of these special three-night Disney convention packages, each including:

- Three nights at a deluxe Walt Disney World Resort (Contemporary or Grand Floridian).
  - Disney Theme Park ticket, good at the Magic Kingdom, Epcot and Disney-MGM Studios from November 14-17.
    - Welcome reception.
    - Admission to all seminars and workshops throughout the event. (Some workshops may require additional fee.)
    - Admission to private sale of limited-edition items.
    - Admission to event auction.
    - Admission to 1996 breakfast awards ceremony.
    - Lunch coupon good at one of many Walt Disney World restaurants.
  - Admission to grand finale party.

Package prices begin at just $698 per person, based on adult double occupancy at Disney's Contemporary Resort, Garden Wing.

Rooms are limited, but the fun isn't, so please call now.

For reservations and information, phone (407) 827-7600
or your travel agent.

Walt Disney World.
Make the dream come true.™

Mickey Mouse Club and local people with whom they deal on a daily basis.

John relates the story of how a lady approached him one day with a small trunk full of Disney items. She had been told that John would offer her a fair price and would prize the items. John, feeling privileged, purchased the Disney items from the trunk. The lady explained how, grief-stricken by the death of her beloved 6-year-old daughter, she had closed the trunk and stored it in her attic.

Now, years later, she wanted John to have the contents. John assured the dear lady they would always have an honored place in his home. She still remains friends with the Andersons and visits them on occasion.

This winning Colorado couple not only formed the first Mickey Mouse Club outside Los Angeles, they have also launched a number of youngsters as Disney collectors—sometimes purchasing the children's first collectibles. Yvonne believes that collecting Disneyana has kept both of them young, and that

Disney collectors and artists have both a look of love in their eyes and a great sense of humor.

Artists

More recently, John and Yvonne have become friends with Alice and Marc Davis. Marc, one of the "Nine Old Men" who started with Walt Disney, is responsible for creating the villains as well as a host of other characters who appear in rides at the Disney theme parks. Of special interest to doll collectors, Marc's wife, Alice, also highly talented, designed and dressed the dolls of Small World and designed the costumes for the Pirates of the Caribbean attractions at Disney parks.

Film History

Disney's early efforts at animation included more than 120 short films of Mickey Mouse and some 126 films of Donald Duck, Pluto, Figaro and Goofy. Once Mickey Mouse and his girlfriend gained popularity, Disney quickly recognized that the public loved the fantasy of little animated characters with humanlike behavior and voices. He also realized they liked characters that reflected the era and the culture in which they were living. Indeed,

Seiberling Latex Products Co. of Akron, Ohio, produced these Three Little Pigs (also found in the lady's trunk) and the Big Bad Wolf in 1934. Because such rubber character dolls were extremely fragile, most of them have melted. The Big Bad Wolf is in more typical condition.

Snow White and the Seven Dwarfs were manufactured in 1938 by Richard G. Krueger, Inc., New York. The dwarfs are made of a washable sharkskin-grain material and velvet. They were produced by both the Krueger and the Ideal Novelty & Toy companies.

audiences were carried away with The Big Bad Wolf, whom they interpreted as symbolic of the Depression from which almost everyone was suffering. The Big Bad Wolf (and the Depression) could huff and puff all it wanted, but it would certainly be chased away.

Disney Items

Not only did the audiences of the 1930s flock to see Disney movies, they were eager to have the dolls based on his characters, as well as watches and other items that were made available to the public in stores.

By the late 1930s, Disney was animating human figures and producing full-length films like *Snow White and the Seven Dwarfs* and *Bambi*. Again, dolls and other Disney items offered as a byproduct of these films were quickly purchased. During the 1940s and 1950s, he produced more feature-length films, including such favorites as *Pinocchio*, *Dumbo* and *Fantasia*, in which highly stylized cartoon figures and color patterns danced to the music of great classical composers.

Then, during the 1950s, Disney produced a series of animated romances and classic fairy tales like *Cinderella*, *Alice in Wonderland* and *Peter Pan*. TV productions of *Davy Crockett* and *Zorro* followed, exciting public interest not only in dolls, but in the coonskin caps and period clothing the characters wore as well.

The list of Disney's achievements goes on and on, with *Mary Poppins, Sleeping Beauty* and other popular figures from the movies by those names taking their places as the dolls which captivated yet another generation of children—and collectors like John and Yvonne Anderson.

It is to Disney's credit that as his career culminated, he helped establish the California Institute of the Arts, or CalArts, in Southern California, where young people are trained to use the arts in a cross-disciplinary manner. **DW**

This highly prized Mickey Mouse is the first thing John would save if his house caught fire. It was produced in 1935 by the Knickerbocker Toy Co. of New York and advertised in the Kay Kamen Character Merchandise Catalog.

All photos courtesy of Marjorie Raizman.

The Most Beautiful Collector
Available Exclusively from

MADAME MARGUERITE
From Maryse Nicole, a creation of exquisite beauty...capturing an era of neverending elegance.
19" (48 cm) $295 Order # 912

MARILYN MONROE IN THE SEVEN YEAR ITCH
Marilyn in her most unforgettable pose.
16" (41 cm) $195 Order # 877

To Order, Use the Attached Card or
Franklin Heirloom Dolls

Dolls in The World...
Franklin Heirloom Dolls.

COLLEEN OF COUNTY CORK
An exquisite musical collector doll.
Plays "When Irish Eyes are Smiling."
19" (48 cm) $195 Order # 637

BLUSHING ROSE
The first-ever heirloom doll in
Maryse Nicole's Premier Signature
Collection. 20" (51 cm)
$495 Order # 874

SOPHISTICATED LADY
A glamorous 60th anniversary tribute from
the world-famous Duke Ellington
Orchestra. 17" (43 cm) $195 Order # 693

DANNY—THE LIMITED EDITION
COCA-COLA® COLLECTOR DOLL
Authorized by The Coca-Cola Company. With
his own scooter. 19" (48 cm) $195 Order # 94

HEATHER
From Maryse Nicole, a turn-of-the-
century treasure lavished with
old-world charm.
10" (25 cm) $135 Order # 415

PEANUT
An original
from Maryse
Nicole's
endearing Tiny
Tot Signature
Collection.
10" (25 cm)
$110
Order # 816

Call Toll-Free 1-800 THE MINT
Franklin Center, PA 19091-0001

The Creations of Original Paper Doll Artist Charles Ventura

By Karen B. Kurtz

We welcome an old friend back to the pages of Doll World.

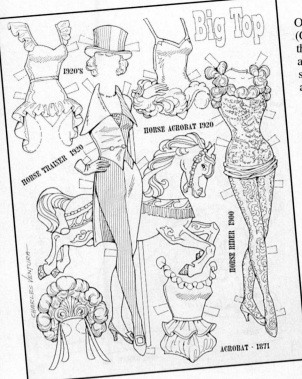

In 1970, *Doll World* published a Charles Ventura paper doll. Interestingly, this event marked the first sale of a Ventura design to a magazine. Since then, Ventura has published periodically with us and our sister publications *Quilt World* and the former *Doll Designs*, as well as other nationally recognized magazines. We are pleased to share the unique talent of a good friend with you again.

First Paper Dolls
During the Great Depression, young Charles Ventura drew costumes for paper dolls. "In those pre-television days," Ventura said, "entertainment was hard to come by, so Mother asked me to draw pictures for my sister, who was confined to her bed for a few months. Of course, all Mary wanted were outfits for her paper dolls!

"After a while I was bored with this task, so I started to draw about 30 pages of costumes in one sitting. Then I hid them away, giving Mary only two or three pages a day. This arrangement worked out well for both of us."

Even after Mary recovered from her illness, she wanted more costumes for her paper dolls, so Ventura kept designing until her collection filled 17 boxes! He remembers designing 100 costumes at once, a practice that made it easier to meet stringent deadlines later in his artistic career.

Nationally known as one of the most prolific pen-and-ink artists around, Ventura, now 70 years old, has created thousands of paper dolls over a 50-year span. Of the 120 paper-doll books he has produced, only one is in full color: *Paper Dolls in the Style of Mucha* (Hobby House Press, 1990). A member of the Original Paper Doll Artists Guild (OPDAG), Ventura has created more than 100 paper dolls for conventions and paper doll parties, and has designed and constructed costumes for a Broadway musical.

Ventura enjoys the "diversion" of making paper dolls for family members. His own daughters, Catherine and Elizabeth, "ignored costumes that came with the commercial paper dolls books, but saved and used my outfits," he said. "I think they were fond of the paper dolls because we did them together. Often I submitted designs named after them to comic strips such as *Katy Keene*, *Jane Arden* or *Winnie Winkle*."

Schooling
Ventura's supple, long-limbed beauties led him to a scholarship at the School of The Art Institute, Chicago, in 1944. "In a dress design course we were required to create costumes for the school fashion show," he said. "Since I didn't know how to sew, Mother made the outfits, and two of them won honorable mentions.

"The instructor encouraged me to learn more about ladies' hats, shoes and purses, so I went to Marshall Field's department store to look at clothes. When I saw that I was the only young man in a woman's world, I thought, *What am I doing here?* and promptly dropped the class."

He persevered in higher education and made a livelihood teaching art and mechanical drawing in Minnesota and the Chicago public schools. While teaching, he moonlighted by designing greeting cards, book jackets, brochures and other commissioned works. Ventura describes his foray into commercial art as "boring," but by this time his creative paper-doll artwork had attracted the attention of nationally known newspaper cartoonists.

Comics
"I deluged Dale Messick, the artist who created *Brenda Starr* for the *Chicago Tribune,* with about 1,500 designs," he said, "and she published some of them. Thirty years later when Brenda Starr got married, I sent her more designs. She published a wedding dress in the January 1, 1976, strip, and later sent me an autographed invitation to Brenda Starr's wedding.

"She also wanted to meet me, so my 14-year-old daughter and I visited her studio in the Loop," he said. "We watched her illustrate the comic strip and glimpsed Brenda Starr's adventures six weeks ahead of everyone else. She gave my daughter an original strip and we also looked at her family albums."

The acclamation Charles received from Dale Messick whetted his appetite for more. He went on to publish paper dolls in *Boots and Her Buddies, Moon Mullins, Dixie Dugan, Teena, Tillie the Toiler, Tiny Tim, Winnie Winkle, Maggie and Jiggs, Buck Rogers* and many other comic strips.

After Ventura's six children left home for college or marriage, he had more time for project development. In 1970, he submitted a paper doll to *Doll World* and it was accepted. It wasn't long until collectors clamored for books of his paper doll art.

"I hadn't planned on doing this, but I drew up some paper doll sets and advertised them," he said. "Four sheets of paper dolls cost $2 then. Hundreds of people ordered them so I drew more and more and more. I have written to thousands of collectors through the years, but I haven't attended any paper doll conventions."

Inspiration
Ventura draws inspiration for new costume ideas from various sources. "I am working now on an idea for the paper doll convention in Detroit," he said. "The theme is 'Fabulous Fashions of Motown,' which makes me think of Motown records and The Supremes and the music that came out of Motown in the 1960s and 1970s.

Continued on page 23

RESERVATION CERTIFICATE

Classic BARBIE™ Ornaments

Please Respond Promptly

YES, please enter my reservation for the *Classic BARBIE™ Ornament Collection,* a division of the Ashton-Drake Heirloom Ornaments Club. Reservation subject to acceptance.

I understand that I need **SEND NO MONEY NOW.** I will pay the first installment of $19.45* for the first 3-ornament set before shipment, and the balance in one monthly installment of $19.45,* *shipping included*. The following sets will be shipped one every two months, each payable in two installments.

X ____________________
Signature   Date

____________________ ( ) ____________________
Name (please print clearly)   Telephone

____
Address   Apt. No.

____
City   State   Zip

*Includes $3.94 home delivery fee per 3-ornament set; add applicable state sales tax.Six to eight weeks delivery.

43337-D45801

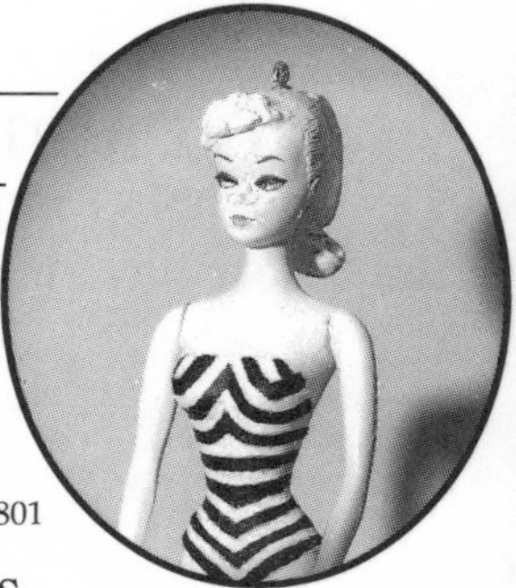

THE ASHTON-DRAKE GALLERIES
9200 North Maryland Avenue, Niles, Illinois 60714-9853

BUSINESS REPLY MAIL

FIRST-CLASS MAIL   PERMIT NO. 90049   CHICAGO, IL

POSTAGE WILL BE PAID BY ADDRESSEE

THE ASHTON-DRAKE GALLERIES
9200 NORTH MARYLAND AVENUE
NILES IL 60714-9853

in this exciting collection, available only by mail.

BARBIE is a trademark owned by and
used under license from Mattel, Inc.
©1995 Mattel, Inc.
All Rights Reserved.
Ornaments made in Indonesia;
display made in U.S.A.

Start your collection with three
famous BARBIE™ doll fashions
from the late 1950s and early 1960s:

• "1959 Original Swimsuit"
  ensemble (shown at right)

• "Enchanted Evening" ensemble
  (pink evening gown with white
  "fur" stole)

• "Gay Parisienne" ensemble
  (navy "bubble" dress with
  white "fur" stole).

Kellogg's Dolls Are Just G-r-r-eat!

When someone mentions Kellogg's cereals it is easy to remember Snap, Crackle and Pop or Tony the Tiger, but the list is much longer. In fact they are probably the king of cereal companies in terms of 20th century ad dolls.

At one time or another they have offered dolls such as Howdy Doody, Woody Woodpecker, Baby Chris, Banana Splits, Magic Mary and Toucan Sam. Kellogg's even came up with a Barbie® Miss America doll produced by Mattel.

In *Advertising Dolls*, Joleen Robison and Key Sellers point out that Kellogg's offered 90 different premium dolls between 1925 and 1978; they stopped counting after that.

Beginnings

The Kellogg's story began in the 1890s when brothers John and Will Keith developed a flaked cereal for patients at the Battle Creek (Mich.) Sanitarium. By 1904, the grain-based product was being manufactured in 40 different factories and sold nationwide.

The firm was officially named the Kellogg Company in 1922 and within a few years had its first ad doll. The premier Goldilocks series included sheets of fabric printed in full color. Four characters of various sizes were available—Goldilocks, Mama Bear, Daddy Bear and Johnny Bear.

In 1928 Kellogg's followed with a Nursery Rhyme series which included Red Riding Hood, Little Bo Peep, Mary and her lamb and Tom the Piper's Son.

Snap, Crackle & Pop

The fabled Snap, Crackle and Pop characters were introduced during the 1930s. They didn't arrive together, however. Snap and his baker's hat were around for several years before they were joined by Crackle in his stocking cap and Pop in his military cap.

By the late 1940s, Snap, Crackle and Pop were available on printed fabric to be sewn into cloth dolls. The price was 15 cents and one box top. The trio were offered as puppet premiums in 1950 and as full-size 16" cloth dolls in 1955. (The cloth doll offer was repeated several times over the next 10 years.)

1950s

Meanwhile, Kellogg's unveiled the delightful Tony the Tiger (my personal favorite) who said of Frosted Flakes, "They're g-r-r-eat!" Tony was an immediate success.

Although offered many times over the years, one of the best Tony dolls was the 14" cloth doll of the 1970s. It was bright orange and came with the traditional neckerchief.

During the 1950s Kellogg's also offered a number of conventional dolls as premiums. Among them were 16" vinyl Sweetheart Doll, the Majorette Doll and Baby Ginger. The company also promoted both vinyl and cloth Howdy Doody dolls.

1960s & Beyond

In the 1960s, there was another run of conventional dolls. Baby Chris was available for $2 and two box tops. Others were Linda Lou, Valerie, Magic Mary and Calico Lassie.

One of the biggest hits in animated characters was Toucan Sam, based on the Froot Loops mascot. Sam was available to the public in both vinyl and cloth forms.

Toucan Sam and the Rice Krispies guys got together in 1984 when Talbot Toys sold all four 5" figures in individual boxes at retail stores. That same year the four figures were also sold as a series of bathtub toys seated in rowboats.

Among the other comic character issues from Kellogg's during the 1960s were Hillbilly Goat, Woody Woodpecker and the Banana Splits which included Snorky, Drooper, Fleegle and Bingo.

In 1972 Kellogg's reached still another level with a Barbie® Miss America doll made by Mattel. The premium price was a modest $3. Thus Kellogg's has earned the title of one of America's most prolific commercial users of advertising and promotion dolls. **DW**

Readers' Questions

In most pictures, Buddy Lee dolls are wearing denim caps and overalls. My doll is wearing a white Coca-Cola uniform. Is it worth more?
D.A., Blue Island, Ill.

Yes, original Buddy Lee dolls in Coke uniforms can be worth up to 50 percent more than the regular ones. Beware of reproductions, however. Most of the true Buddy Lees were made from composition or very hard plastic.

My doll has a cap which says "Freddy Fast." We think it may have been used for a brand of aspirin.
P.H., Greenville, Ky.

Freddy Fast was a character for the Douglas Oil Company. Plastic dolls were distributed at service stations in the 1970s. In good condition they list in the $20–$25 range.

We have a disagreement over this cloth Popeye doll. It is 15" tall, and I say it was sold in stores. My friend says it was an advertising doll at one time. What do you say?
S.D., Raytown, Mo.

You may both be right. A Popeye ad doll was offered in the 1970s by the makers of Popeye Puffed Wheat/Rice and Popeye Popcorn. It required a package coupon and a small amount of cash. These dolls may also have been retailed by the manufacturer at some point.

Send your brief questions on advertising dolls to columnist Robert Reed at P.O. Box 204, Knightstown, IN 46148.

A Special Message from a Heavenly Angel

Love Is Patient

By

Phyllis Parkins

The Hamilton Collection — BETTER QUALITY · BETTER VALUE

Only $29.95!

- **Highly detailed, hand-painted porcelain**
- **Includes book bearing a special message**

Love is Patient

Shown smaller than actual size of 5" high

Patience is a virtue, especially if you're a special messenger from heaven above. But it doesn't always come easily. It's apparent that even this toe-tapping spiritual guardian finds being patient a bit difficult at times!

Now, acclaimed doll artist Phyllis Parkins has created her very first doll sculpture with "Love Is Patient." This enchanting new work of art is meticulously sculpted in the finest porcelain and lovingly hand-painted in inviting pastel hues. With soft blue eyes, fanciful "real" feathery wings and a halo of silk flowers, this adorable little angel silently offers words of encouragement.

"Love Is Patient" premieres the *Little Messengers* Doll Sculpture Collection, featuring sweet cherubs bestowing messages of love and kindness. As an owner, you will have the right—without obligation—to preview all subsequent works in the collection. What's more, our 30 Day *100% Satisfaction Guarantee* assures you order without risk. So send in your order today!

©1996 HC. All Rights Reserved.

KERRA'S KUT-OUTS

By Kerra Davis

New and longtime collectors will find helpful tips to paper doll collecting.

Welcome to the world of paper dolls!

Paper dolls have become one of the fastest-growing areas in collecting. And why not? Their appeal is obvious, they require little space and their cost is reasonable when compared to other collectibles.

There are a multitude of choices for the collector. Examples do exist from the 17th and 18th centuries, but these are very expensive and rarely seen outside museums and private collections. Nineteenth and 20th century versions, however, are not only available, they are quite affordable in most cases. (Think how many paper dolls you could get for the price of one French fashion doll.)

Narrow Your Choices

Some collectors zero in on one area such as a certain time frame, artist or company. Paper dolls by American McLoughlin Brothers or those by Raphael Tuck of England would make large collections by themselves.

There are advertising paper dolls, magazine paper dolls, and dolls in newspapers, books and boxes. Represented are famous people, occupations, babies, families, weddings, cowboys; and this list could go on and on.

Some are stationary, some are articulated. There are those with "real" hair and those with eyes which open and shut. There are animals—almost any kind you can think of.

Probably some of the paper dolls most popular with collectors today are those representing the movie stars of the 1940s and 1950s, not to mention the many television sitcom examples.

There are a number of good books providing the collector with years of research at her fingertips. These should be studied and enjoyed so that the collector will know just how she wants to go about beginning and adding to her collection.

Where to Look

Paper dolls are everywhere, often in surprising places. Old magazines and newspapers frequently have paper dolls. Boxes of paper ephemera sometimes contain envelopes of these treasures, and books were a favorite keeping place. Albums of scrap pictures can yield paper dolls, and framed examples are not uncommon.

Following is your own personal road map to the world of paper dolls and successful collecting. Have fun and enjoy the trip.

1. Decide where you are going. Where do you want to be when you reach the end

The beginning of Kerra's paper doll collection. Saved from her childhood, this is Mimi with disk eyes that flicker and four outfits that snap onto the snap at her neck. She is from the late 1950s–early 1960s.

of your journey? Do you want to be in a place with all types of paper dolls, or will you be happier with specialization?

2. Read and study the map. A collection becomes a real part of you when you know what you are doing. Books about paper dolls are a great place to start. Get involved with others who enjoy paper dolls and learn from them. Subscribe to paper doll publications.

3. How much luggage can you handle? As with any journey, be realistic about the space you have. It is true that paper dolls take very little room, but how much "little" room do you have? Will you display them all, or will you be content to have special items packed?

4. Is it a family trip? Most of us do not live alone. A collection cannot be fun unless it is accepted by the whole family. They may not collect what you do—they may not collect at all—but don't ever let a hobby cause problems. Paper doll collecting should be fun!

5. How much can you spend? This is probably one of the most important decisions ever made with a collection. Decide how much money can be spent comfortably on your passion. Then stick to the decision. Avoid going over budget because you must have that paper doll. You'll not be happy with yourself in the morning. If it's too expensive right now, wait and save.

6. Be accepting of second-class accommodations. Face the facts. Hobbyists have to realize what they can and can't have. Most collectors cannot afford paper dolls in the hundreds of dollars. Don't let it bother you. Be happy with what you can have.

7. Remember the film! Keep records. Record the buying of that paper doll. Take its picture; note how much it cost and where you got it. Write down any history that is known—it will be important in the future.

8. Share the memories. As you take your journey and learn along the way, be ready to share what you know with interested others. By telling and sharing, you just might be the one to start them on a paper doll journey. **DW**

Kerra welcomes your questions about paper dolls; selected letters will be answered in this column. A photograph or slide will help in identification. For return, enclose SASE. Kerra Davis, 1779 Mershon Rd., Mershon, GA 31551.

A day you will always remember.
A bride you could never forget.

ROMANTIC ROSE BRIDE™ BARBIE®

 A bouquet of roses. A veil of lace. A love that will last forever.

Introducing Romantic Rose Bride Barbie doll. As part of the elegant Wedding Flower Collection,™ this porcelain bride celebrates the beauty and romance of wedding flowers.

Romantic Rose Bride Barbie is as graceful and lovely as the flower she's named for. Her lavish, appliquéd bodice and sleeves are dotted with roses and hand-sewn faux pearls. Her exquisite train, accented with ribbon rosettes, is patterned after delicate antique lace and swirls gently around her ivory, satin skirt. Her auburn hair is swept up demurely, and in her hands, she holds a bouquet of delicate, handcrafted roses.

Romantic Rose Bride is a numbered, Limited Edition doll, handpainted and hand-crafted entirely of fine bisque porcelain.

Complete with Certificate of Authenticity, you can acquire her now only through direct subscription for 5 easy payments of $35.80.

Romantic Rose Bride Barbie. A perfect portrait of love.

IDENTIFYING YOUR DOLLS ✪ BY LAUREN JAEGER

Play Dolls

Doll A is marked "Alex" and measures 7½". It is hard plastic with jointed knees, but I don't know if the clothes are original.

Doll B is soft plastic and has a one-piece body. When the belly is squeezed she squeaks and her pigtails jump up. She is wearing her original dress and barrettes, and measures 14" tall. She is marked on the head "Ideal Toy Corp.//Hong Kong, 1978, 298."

Doll C is 13½" tall, marked "Vogue Doll, c. 1963," and has sleep eyes. She is made of soft plastic.

Jean Johnson, Delaware

Your dolls are good representatives of popular playthings from different decades. Doll A is an Alexander-kins; these dolls were manufactured from 1961–1965 with bent knees, and from 1965–1972 with bent knees and a walker mechanism; the head turns when the legs move in a walking motion. Literally hundreds of different characters were made by the famous Madame Alexander Co. using this model, and it would be very, very difficult, if not impossible, to say who you have without the original clothing. The value would be about $85 without original clothes, and would skyrocket into the hundreds of dollars with the original outfit.

Doll B was a well-publicized doll named Whoopsie, made by Ideal in the late 1970s. The doll appeared in a television commercial which showed the ponytails "in action." It is worth a maximum of $25. Finally, Doll C is Angel Baby, a play doll made by the Vogue Doll Corp. in 1965. Vogue was very well-known for the Ginny series.

Compo & Eugene

Doll A is 21" tall and has a composition head and limbs and a cloth body. She has sleep eyes, two teeth and a red cloth tongue. The head is cracked and peeling on top and around the ears. The lady who gave her to me is 62 years old and got this doll when she was a small child. There are no markings.

Doll B is 20" with vinyl limbs and a cloth body. It is marked "E 61850." The tag on the cloth body says "Eugene Doll Co.//New York, NY." It has real-life details on the hands and feet. The cry box inside the body does not work.

Shirley Gandy, Missouri

Doll A was made by an unknown American manufacturer around 1940. Unfortunately for doll collectors, these unmarked composition baby dolls look so much alike that it is difficult to say who made them. Most likely this doll was made by a larger company, such as Arranbee or Ideal.

The cracks you describe are called "crazing," and were caused by fluctuating weather conditions over the years. The value of the doll with the crazing repaired and dressed is $65.

Doll B was made by the Eugene Doll Co. which specialized in play dolls for younger children. The doll is Just Born, first issued in 1975, but still available in the 1980s. The value is about $25 dressed up beautifully.

Soldier Boy

I am enclosing photographs of a charming doll my daughter rescued from a garbage can. He is composition and his clothes are his body. He wears a brown twill uniform and black twill boots and has a holster, backpack and ditty bag.

His brass buttons have little anchors on them. His pistol is made of lead. The paint on the bright blue eyes has worn out and he has a craze line on the head.

Doris S. Saunders, New York

This is a charming soldier boy made by an unknown American doll manufacturer in the early 1920s. The value, if in mint condition, would be about $125. As is, the value would be about half that.

Toddles, Betsy Wetsy & Toni

I received these dolls from my cousin, and she is in her late 40s. She just didn't want them anymore, and they had been in her grandmother's attic for years. Some were originally her dolls, while others had belonged to her aunt.

Doll A is a 7½" composition doll with painted features. The clothes are tagged "Vogue Dolls, Inc. Medford, Mass" and on the back of the doll is marked "Vogue."

Doll B is a 12" vinyl baby doll marked "Ideal Doll, WC-1-1." She has a hole in the mouth for a bottle. Doll C is hard plastic and marked "Ideal." She came with no clothes, just ice skates. I know she is a Toni but I would like to know the value.

Faye Albertson, Texas

Doll A is Toddles, which was made by the Vogue Doll Corp. in the 1950s. This is a very interesting doll, since she was the predecessor of a much more famous doll named Ginny which looked almost identical to Toddles but was of hard plastic. Virginia Graves designed this little doll, and was the mastermind behind the Ginny doll, as well. The value is about $150.

Doll B is Betsy Wetsy made by Ideal in 1959. The drink-and-wet doll was first made by Ideal in the 1930s and, like its cousin, Dye-Dee, caused a flurry of controversy. The value of this doll is about $40.

Doll C is Toni, one of the prettiest hard-plastic dolls ever made by Ideal in the 1950s. You did not tell me the size of the doll, but her value would begin at $100.

Dream Baby

This 23" doll has a composition head marked "Dream Baby" and blue sleep eyes. I inherited this doll from my grandmother, so I believe it to date from 1930–1940.

Teri Wertman, Hawaii

This is Dream Baby made by the Arranbee Doll Corporation in the 1930s. An earlier, more valuable bisque-head version of this doll was made by Armand Marseille of Germany specifically for Arranbee. Your doll is typical of the fat mama-baby dolls that were made throughout the 1920s and 1930s by different American manufacturers. The value of the doll is about $185.

Fashion Dolls

Can you tell me about the following dolls? The one on the left has blond hair, is 20" tall and has hazel eyes. The arms are hard plastic. The tag on the dress says "Miss Revlon 1958" and "Ideal." The head is marked "14 R." The doll on the right is 21", marked "21HH K88." The legs and body are of rigid plastic.

Ruth Emerson, New York

The doll on the right is Candy Fashion made in 1962 by Deluxe. Candy Fashion was originally boxed with several glamorous outfits and dress forms to display them. Although the doll on the left wears an authentic dress for an Ideal Revlon doll, these lady dolls marked "14 R" were made by several American doll companies in the 1950s.

It is often thought that Ideal marketed the 14 R doll as a Mrs. Revlon, the mother of Miss Revlon. The value of Candy Fashion would be about $50, while the 14 R doll, because of the nice dress, would be worth about $70.

Bannister Baby

This doll is marked "Constance Bannister, New York, New York" on the head, and "MFG by The Sun Rubber Co. under one or more U.S. Pat." with several patent numbers listed. The doll has brown molded hair, sleep eyes and black lashes. It measures about 18" tall. I believe it is made out of rubber.

Vicky Kleinfeldt, California

This is the Bannister Baby made in the mid-1950s by the Sun Rubber Company in Ohio. The company made a host of rubber toys and dolls, all of which are valued by collectors today.

Constance Bannister was a famous baby photographer, and her photos were illustrated in the Sunday comics page in the newspaper. The photographs were accompanied by funny captions. The value of the doll is about $65.

Thumbelina & AE

I received Doll A as a Christmas gift from my daughters last year. The doll is marked "Ideal Toy Corp" and was made in 1983. It is 18" tall and has a porcelain head. It says "#1 of a limited edition." Doll B was purchased about one year ago. It is marked "AE 3051 10" and measures 36" tall.

Gloria Orndorff, West Virginia

Doll A was a re-issue of an Ideal classic originally made in the early 1960s. The first Thumbelina was a realistic infant doll with automation inside which made it wriggle like a newborn. Your doll was issued to take advantage of the booming collector's market. As such, these dolls were kept in pristine condition, since they were expensive to purchase when new. The value is about $200.

The black doll, I must say, is difficult to date but may be from the late 1960s. It is a Patti Playpal-type, or a companion doll, which means it could wear the clothing of a 3-year-old child. The doll, if it is indeed nearly 30 years old, would be worth about $250. The "AE" marking belongs to the doll manufacturer/wholesaler Allied Eastern.

Continued on page 22

Celebrate her precious homecoming, because she's your very own ...

"Beautiful Newborn"

A delicate portrait of a new-born baby girl with her own knitted layette by artist Yolanda Bello

Affordably priced at

only **$49**⁹⁵ *plus shipping*

That's Ashton-Drake value!

Unconditionally guaranteed for one full year, or your money back (including postage)!

*N*estled in her pink-and-white layette, this new baby is ready to meet the world, though she's just a few days old. Reach out and touch her rounded cheeks, with the rosy glow of a newborn's skin ... her long, curled fingers ... her tiny toes! She's "Beautiful Newborn," the first issue in the *Miracle of Life* collection by Yolanda Bello. This "Beautiful Newborn" is hand-crafted in porcelain and hand-painted. She comes with her own delicately-knitted four-piece layette and satin-edged receiving blanket. "Beautiful Newborn" is an exclusive edition too precious to miss! So don't let this opportunity pass you by. She's yours for just $49.95, payable in 3 monthly installments of $18.30 (shipping included). To bring this sweet little one home, order today.

THE ASHTON-DRAKE GALLERIES
Bringing You Dolls of Irresistible Value

93681-CC3AR

BUSINESS REPLY MAIL

FIRST- CLASS MAIL   PERMIT NO. 90049   CHICAGO,IL

POSTAGE WILL BE PAID BY ADDRESSEE

THE ASHTON-DRAKE GALLERIES
9200 NORTH MARYLAND AVENUE
NILES IL 60714-9853

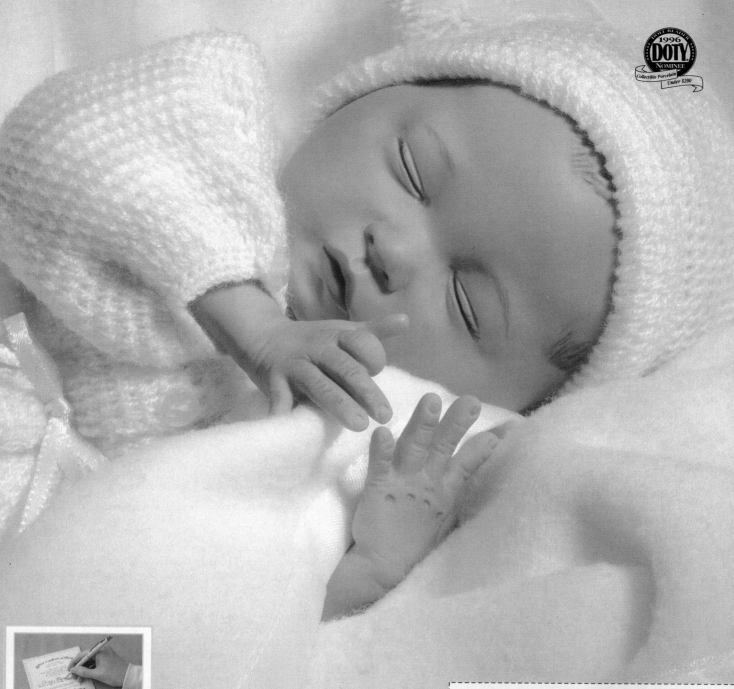

Artist Doll

This doll was given to me in 1945 and the woman said it had been in the family for years, yet she didn't know where it came from. I am 61 and I would like to know something about the doll so I could sell it.

The body is made from plaster of paris and she has cloth arms. I'm not sure what the face and hands are made of. The dress is cotton. I have not been able to find another doll like her in the library, and other collectors have not been able to tell me anything.

Callie Norgaar, California

What a wonderful mystery! Certainly this was a handmade doll, dating to about 1939 when *Gone With the Wind* was all the rage. I do not know who the doll artist was, but you own a unique and very, very valuable piece of Americana.

Dolly Face

This beautiful doll is 18" tall and has a kid body, bisque head and blue glass eyes. She has four teeth. The mark on the back of the head is "W & C" and it has a horseshoe-type stamp.

Bernette Albert, Maine

The doll was made by a little-known firm named Wiefel and Company, and dates to about 1912. This is a typical German doll with a blank expression known as a "dolly-faced" doll. In excellent shape, the value would be about $550.

China Head

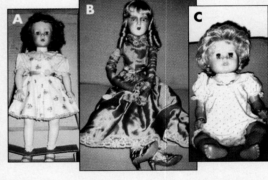

This doll was left to me by my great-grandmother who died at age 98 when I was 7. I'm now 61. I understand that Great-Grandmother brought this doll from Austria, where she had played with it when she was very young. The doll is 24" tall and has a china head. She wears her original clothing.

Shirley Smith, Pennsylvania

Your china-head doll was made in Germany around 1870. Besides being a one-owner doll, which adds considerably to its value (collectors love to know where their things came from, who originally owned them, etc.), the doll is in excellent condition. It is of beautiful quality china and has brown eyes, which are difficult to find. Most china dolls have painted blue eyes.

The hairstyle is difficult to pinpoint from the dark photo, but it appears to be a flat-top china with a row of ringlets around the head. If so, the value of the doll would be at least $700. The value of a china-head doll is determined by rarity of the hairstyle, as well as quality.

American & German

My son sent me Doll A for Christmas. She is a 30" walker wearing original clothing and still in the original box. The box is marked "American Character Doll." She has a hard-plastic body and legs, soft, original arms and head, blue sleep eyes and a closed mouth. It looks like this doll has never been out of the box.

Doll B is 26" tall, all-original except for the new wig, and is marked "T." Doll C is 20" tall with light blue sleep eyes. She is marked "Made in West Germany."

Theresa Larsen, Kansas

Doll A is Sweet Sue, one of the most successful fashion dolls ever made. As marked, she was made by the American Character Doll Corp. The doll, which came in several heights wearing a large assortment of fashions, was first manufactured in the 1950s. Your example dates to 1960. In this mint, original condition, the doll is worth about $550.

Doll B is a good example of a boudoir doll dating to the 1920s or 1930s. These dolls were made by several American and European companies, and were meant to be used as decorative pieces, not as playthings. The value is about $125.

Finally, Doll C was made by the well-known German doll manufacturer Zapf and it dates to about 1972. The value is about $50–$75.

Scarlett O'Hara

This doll is 50 years old and was called Scarlett O'Hara. She is 20" tall and the body and face are composition. The hair feels real, but has become matted over the years. She has pantaloons and buckled shoes. I received her on my 12th birthday.

Beatrice Stem, Massachusetts

This doll does resemble Scarlett O'Hara with her black hair, green eyes and Southern belle costume. She was, no doubt, meant to represent the famous Margaret Mitchell character. However, your doll is not the licensed Scarlett made by the Madame Alexander Doll Corp., which looks quite different from your doll.

Although your doll is American-made, probably made by Arranbee (she looks like Nancy), she is not Scarlett. The value, however, because of the excellent condition and fine quality, is $350. **DW**

Charles Ventura

Continued from page 11

"I will probably look for a figure for the doll in a magazine or newspaper," Ventura continued, "and then draw the doll in appropriate undergarments. If I have drawn the doll too large, I will reduce the image in a copy machine. Then I'll place the reduced drawing on my light box and redraw it," he said.

He can design and draw a paper doll book in three weeks if research isn't required. He begins the research process by first checking his own library for costumes of the '60s, or he may go to the library to "sketch, sketch, sketch."

"After I have researched a few costume ideas," he continued, "I'll place tracing paper over the finished doll on the light box and draw the costume. When I have 10 or 15 pages of designs on tissue, I'll select the best of them for the book. Sometimes my enthusiasm is excessive and I'll end up with too many finished pages. When that happens, I have hard choices to make, discarding some but keeping only the very best sketches."

Collectors consider Ventura's strengths his simplicity and sureness of line that produces very detailed drawings.

Always Improving

As Charles Ventura nears the end of a very full artistic life, he still amuses himself by designing special paper dolls for granddaughters Marie and Anya. (*Anya's Garden* was featured in *Contemporary Doll Collector*, August 1993.)

He also strives to "constantly improve the drawing. At 70, I just don't have the energy I had 10 years ago," he said. "If I'm not alert and concentrating, my work is sloppy. I want to draw figures more accurately. The work of other artists is a benchmark, investigating how to draw different materials, how fabric is draped, or how reflections from sequined gowns fall. But I do think that all of my efforts show.

"Recently, I looked through some old files and saw how I avoided drawing hands," he said. "Now when hands are needed, I will draw them by looking at a photograph or art book to see how they are positioned."

Charles Ventura, a shy, reclusive man, has truly enriched our lives by his wonderfully distinctive artwork, and his legacy will live on in the hearts of paper doll collectors for years to come. **DW**

For more information, contact Charles Ventura at Box 12192, Merrillville, IN 46411.

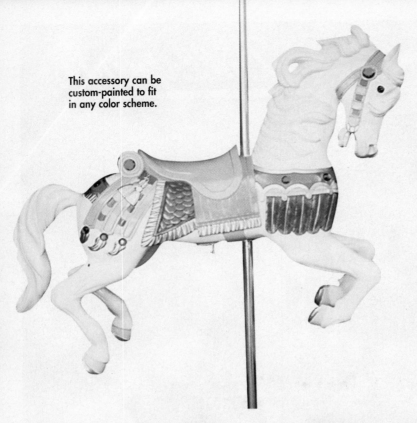

Dolls & Horses Are Perfect Companions

By Shirley Knox

Are your dolls crowded on a shelf? Could they use a new look and some action in their lives? Take them for a carousel ride.

The conventional manner of displaying dolls is in a crowded showcase or shelf. Space permitting, they would look better under less-crowded conditions.

Displaying a favorite doll in a lively and interesting way is not new. Dolls are often displayed holding a favorite toy or another doll. They may also be seated in a high chair, buggy or playpen. Miniature doll strollers with elaborate filigree work are typically Victorian.

An Oriental doll may be seated on a throne-back chair near a richly carved pedestal table. Folding screens and hand-stitched and embroidered silk tapestries add appeal. During the Christmas holidays dolls look very sweet seated on a sleigh next to the tree.

Creating the Horses

Jan Knight, carousel horse artist, gives us a new, wonderful way to enjoy our dolls. Jan has been interested in horses since childhood and painted her first on canvas at age 11. She studied art in college and is busy making a lifelong dream come true by painting carousel horses. The horses are molded from polyethylene, and mold marks and seams must be cleaned and sanded, then treated with an undercoating before the artist begins a design.

Each carousel horse is unique. Even the same color combination is different, as Jan mixes the paint. Colors may be from a fabric swatch, wallpaper or other items where the carousel horse is to be displayed. Jan mixed paint for a friend to match her doll's clothing.

She adds rhinestones for interest. Other designs are made to the individual order. Molded clay roses are handmade, created personally by Jan to add a special touch; others are painted directly onto the horse. She paints feathers onto some palomino horses for a Western effect. She also uses braiding and tassels.

Lifelike Features

White horses are most popular, but Jan uses beige, tan, brown, black and gray as well. Because of her early experience of training and showing horses and her artistic training, Jan is able to carefully paint the eyes. They are so lifelike they appear to follow you.

Carousel horses may also be ordered with music boxes. They come in all sizes, from miniature tree ornaments to life-size horses that are strong enough to hold an adult. But the most popular size is the 36" x 27" horse, which works well with most dolls.

The brass pole is coated so it will not tarnish, and needs no special cleaning. The carousel horse is easy to clean. Wipe with a damp cloth, or spray-polish wood.

Jan has also designed a wooden rocking horse named Josie. Jan says the rockers are the tricky part of this horse. They must be perfectly balanced to rock the horse properly. Since it is designed for dolls, a ribbon is needed to hold the doll in place.

These interesting and unique doll accessories fit well into a new or existing collection. Jan's studio is located in the home she built with her husband, Dave. **DW**

You may contact Jan Knight at 8485 Sunshine Grove Rd., Brooksville, FL 34613, (904) 596–4137.

Dolls and carousel horses make perfect companions for showing off details.
Photo courtesy of Shirley Knox.

lieve locations as they can be attached to Starr's white 4 x 4 sports vehicle with working lights and engine.

With the Magic Motion attachment to a runway or set, little girls can make dolls appear to walk on their own merely by rotating the wand on which the doll stands.

Birth of a Supermodel

The legend of Starr's discovery and eventual supermodel status has a very humble beginning. She was discovered quite by chance when she was just a small infant. While her mother was shopping at the local supermarket, a woman from a children's talent agency approached them and said, "That's the most beautiful baby I have ever seen. I'm going to make this child a star!" Thus Starr's modeling career began, and it is also how she got her name.

This is the kind of story which dreams are made of, and little girls learn how Starr's career progressed from diaper commercials to the fashion runways of Paris and magazine covers.

Although Starr is beautiful, little girls can take a lesson from Starr, who inspires them to keep up with good school grades as a priority for a modeling career. (Starr juggled a

busy modeling career around her studies and managed to graduate at the top of her college class.)

The Starr Agency

Starr was not only fascinated with the glamorous end of the business but she also dreamed of owning her own successful modeling agency. So after graduating from college, she decided to open the Starr Model Agency.

Not just an agency for those with beautiful faces, the agency was looking for model wannabes who would live up to the standards of being well-educated, refined and talented. A Starr model had to be special, not just a pretty face. She had to have great model potential with good character and a better-than-average school record.

Supermodel Search

That's why Starr decided to hold a Supermodel Search contest. From the hundreds of girls who turned out for the contest, Starr chose Dawn, Toya, Amber, Taylor and Misty. They were intelligent and uncommonly beautiful, with a special quality that separated them from all the other pretty faces. Each of Starr's supermodel dolls is different, unique in skin tone and eye color. Most important, each model doll has a special talent. Recently, an Asian-American model named Jade was added to the roster of models who make up Starr's agency.

Model Biographies

Each doll is an inspiration for young girls on the verge of growing up and for collectors as well. Each tells a story of achievement and success, and as a play object instills lifestyle values for career planning.

Dawn, the all-American girl, has appeal for the sports-minded young girl who can relate to Dawn's athletic ability and natural beauty. The blond-haired, blue-eyed Dawn's modeling career really took off when she was discovered by a local talent agent at a swim meet. Modeling helped Dawn earn some extra money while she went to school. She is now busy doing swimsuit ads and sportswear commercials in which she shows off her athletic talents.

Tonya, with her jet-black hair and striking light brown eyes, is an up-and-coming star in the music business. Young girls may fulfill their showbiz dreams as they learn from Tonya. She went to college in New York City where she studied all kinds of music from jazz to classical, but she loves to perform the most. As a Starr model,

her calendar is full because she is in demand by fashion magazines and record companies alike.

Amber is a classically beautiful strawberry blonde. She flashes her bright green eyes like the talented actress she is and, like little-girl imitators, she hopes one day to make it on the big screen. Now, thanks to Starr, Amber's dream is being fulfilled as she juggles modeling dates and fashion shoots with movie deals.

Taylor has a natural talent for painting and drawing, but photography is her passion. Taylor decided that getting back into modeling would be a great help to her career as a photographer.

With Taylor's energy and determination, she is bound to be as successful with photography as she is with modeling.

Misty, with her dreams of becoming a famous fashion designer, competed in the Starr supermodel contest in a unique way. The students at her university were called upon to design gowns for the contestants of the Starr Supermodel Search. When Misty met with Starr to show her the designs, Starr was not only impressed by Misty's talent, but her brown-eyed brunette beauty, as well. Today every

magazine wants photographs of Misty and her fashion designs.

Jade, a newcomer to the roster of supermodels, is an Asian-American beauty with gleaming black hair. Her ambition to become a doctor instilled a serious side to her beautiful persona. However, when her friends told her about the Starr Supermodel Search, she took up the challenge as a means of reaching her goal. Starr immediately saw Jade's model potential and now she is booked with modeling assignments that enable her to afford medical school.

What next at the Starr Model Agency? Rumor has it that male model dolls may be added to complete the Starr Model Search. **DW**

Texas State Fair Babies

By Louvinia T. Smith

Visitors to the Texas State Fair bought plates, cups, spoons, banks, pillows and paperweights to commemorate the event. Some collectors went the more personal route and bought a doll—or two!

Everything is big in Texas. It is huge—850 miles in length and breadth. An old jingle reflects the dismay felt by a traveler crossing Texas: "The sun has riz, the sun has set, And here we is, in Texas yet."

To outsiders, Dallas represents Texas. And it is here that the annual state fair is held in State Fair Park.

The Texas State Sesquicentennial Fair in 1986 was no exception as to size. It had the largest state Ferris wheel in the world which has become permanent for all state fairs since. It dominates the skyline in downtown Dallas.

There were seven gigantic exhibition buildings. It took me two or three visits to discover the dolls. Mattel had a display of Barbie® dolls like I've never seen before, including two life-size dolls dressed as the 1986 Peaches 'n' Cream and the brand-new 1986 Magic Moves Barbie.

Baby Dolls

After I finally tore myself away from the Barbie doll display I wandered among the booths displaying every kind of doll imaginable. I am not a baby doll collector—I lean more toward fashion dolls. But when I saw Annie and Benjy they cried out to me, "Buy me! Buy me!" I had to have them in my collection. They are now the only babies in my extensive doll collection.

Annie, an adorable girl baby crafted of the finest quality porcelain, is No. 269 of a 1,000-piece limited edition, produced by the Tarko's Doll Company, the official vendor of Texas Sesquicentennial Commemorative Dolls. She is the first of a series created just for the Texas Sesquicentennial State Fair in 1986. She is dressed in a pale blue print top, ruffled panties and a bonnet, all trimmed with white lace.

Benjy was there as a preview of the 1987 State Fair doll. Benjy is a precious crying boy doll with tears on his cheek, set-in eyes and painted, molded hair. He is dressed in a two-piece hot-pink knit suit with "State Fair of Texas, October 1987, Dallas, Texas," emblazoned across his little chest. He was irresistible; I had to pick him up and comfort him. He, too, is No. 269 of a limited edition of 1,000.

Both of these babies are meticulously handcrafted, each being handled 23 times before completion. Heads, arms and legs are of flawless porcelain bisque and are assembled on a cloth body. Each porcelain piece is individually hand-polished, creating a satin-smooth finish. Skilled artists have painted each face to capture heart-rending expressions.

Souvenirs

State fair souvenirs can be purchased on the spur of the moment without a major dent in the budget. Most are bought and collected to be displayed to show where the family has traveled. The entire field of souvenirs was available, including banks, pillows, plates, cups, paperweights and spoons, but my souvenirs of the Texas State Fair are Annie and Benjy.

Annie and Benjy cost $40 each, which is fairly inexpensive for a finely crafted porcelain doll. I bought them because they appealed to me—not with any thought of them appreciating in value. But I wonder, are they now sought by collectors and commanding a higher price?

I went to the Texas State Fair alone, although I took along two people: my adult self and the tag-along child inside each of us. I returned with four, including my two Texas babies. **DW**

Porcelain dolls make wonderful souvenirs of your state fair visits.

Dolls courtesy of Louvinia Smith.

A-Dopt-the-Dollies
Trading Cards
for
Doll Lovers

2½" x 3½" inch color portraits of
CLASSICAL HEIRLOOM DOLLS

Each unique, colorful card is **numbered** and **features historical facts** along with the estimated **value of the dolls** shown.

An **endless variety** of German, French, American, as well as ethnic costume, Barbie, Shirley Temple and classical dolls are shown with original props and accessories.

Collect all 63 of these beautiful cards in this limited, first edition.

Each pack contains ten different cards— comes attractively mounted on your choice of an original art doll (10" high), shown on the left or below.

CARD FRONTS
(Shown smaller than actual size)

Art Doll "A"

Clip & mail this order form

Mail to:
A-dopt-the-Dollies
P.O. Box 5611
Somerset, NJ 08873
(tel) 908-422-3173

™

Art Doll "B"

NAME

ADDRESS

CITY   STATE   ZIP

Description (Art Doll "A" or "B")	Quantity x	Price each =	Total
		$3.95	
		$3.95	

Price: **$3.95 per pack**

	Subtotal
New Jersey residents please add 6% sales tax	
Postage & Handling See chart at left	
TOTAL enclosed	

POSTAGE & HANDLING
For orders totaling: Add:
Up to $4.99........... $2.25
Up to $9.99........... $2.95
Up to $15.99.......... $3.95
Up to $24.99.......... $4.50
$25 and up............. $4.95

No cash or CODs.
Orders for delivery to Canada please add $1 per item to postage and handling. U.S. funds only.
No orders outside U.S. and Canada.

Yuko Green © 93

Miniature Dolls & Dollhouses at Williamsburg

By Beth Wheeler

A visit to the Abby Aldrich Rockefeller Folk Art Center at Colonial Williamsburg has a lot to offer doll collectors and dollhouse miniature collectors any time of year—but they're all decked out during the holiday season!

Each Christmas season since 1957, an army of volunteers and staff members has installed an exhibit of fine dollhouses, miniatures and accessories from the collection of the Abby Aldrich Rockefeller Folk Art Center at Colonial Williamsburg in Williamsburg, Va. The Folk Art Center is the first in the United States devoted exclusively to collecting, exhibiting and researching American folk art.

The detail and quality of the 1995 exhibit was so outstanding, a book, *Dollhouses, Miniature Kitchens and Shops* by Susan Hight Rountree, has been published to share some of the wonders with those unable to visit the center personally. Ms. Rountree, who has written two other books about Colonial Williamsburg, is an accomplished miniaturist and craftsperson with intimate knowledge of the exhibit and its details.

Christmas 1995
During the 1995 holiday season, two fully decorated dollhouses were on view as well as several room vignettes, three of which had never before been seen by the public. More than 36,000 visitors to the Folk Art Center had the opportunity to experience the excitement of dollhouse and miniature collecting from Nov. 18, 1995–Jan. 2, 1996.

The Morris-Canby-Rumford Dollhouse, a rare cabinet-style dollhouse filled with original

With its doors closed, the Morris-Canby-Rumford Dollhouse measures 53½" tall, 40" wide, and 21½" deep. This rare cabinet-style dollhouse is painted to resemble a two-story brick dwelling, possibly similar to the Morris family's Philadelphia home. It was built and furnished around 1820 for twin sisters Sarah Wistar Morris and Elizabeth Clifford Morris and remained in the same family until its bequest to Colonial Williamsburg in 1981 with the stipulation that only family members could make changes to the house.

The remarkable kitchen of the Long Island Dollhouse is filled with tiny wonders. Of special interest is the handmade black silk doll, similar to Brazilian rag dolls dated as late as 1930. This unusual doll is stuffed with cotton; details include inserted glass eyes, sculpted facial features, elbows, knees and hips, and tiny pieces of translucent celluloid for fingernails.

The Millinery Shop is a 9⅛" tall x 21¾" wide x 8½" deep free-standing miniature room from the 19th century. The Sonnenberg doll from the 1820s is made from carved wood and features a composition head and shoulders. Other items in the room reflect a variety of dates, creating a mysterious mixture and little documentation.

handcrafted miniatures, and The Long Island Dollhouse, an impressive 12-foot-long Colonial Revival-style structure believed to be one of the longest dollhouses of America from the early 20th century, were the highlights of the show.

A tool shed, three kitchens, a dry goods shop, millinery shop and post office rounded out the exhibit. The Nuremberg kitchen, the dry goods shop and post office had never before been on public view.

The Morris-Canby-Rumford Dollhouse

The Morris-Canby-Rumford Dollhouse is extraordinary for a number of reasons. Its size, furnishings and condition, the quality of the handcrafted furnishings, the fact that the house and furnishings were made by family members and that the house chronicles one family's history are all impressive. The fact that the family history has been cherished and passed from one generation to another and now remains as a model and inspiration is perhaps the most remarkable feature of all.

The cabinet-style house is built of painted yellow pine and poplar with massive hinged doors that open to reveal four well-appointed rooms. The dining room is beautifully furnished with handmade furniture including a tall walnut clock that is a miniature version of a full-size clock that remains in the family today.

The kitchen features a fireplace fitted with a miniature Dutch oven and reflecting oven, as well as other items important to a well-stocked kitchen. The cozy parlor seems a most inviting place for reading, needlework or polite conversation, while the bedroom houses many exquisite accessories.

Several outstanding miniature dolls are found in the rooms. A peg-wooden doll from the 1820s with finely detailed face and "tucked comb" hair is nestled in the parlor

along with a companion more than 100 years her junior. Two 19th century china heads and a tiny jointed doll are found in the bedroom.

The Long Island Dollhouse

The Long Island Dollhouse is an incredible 12 feet long, 6 feet tall and 3½ feet deep! It is constructed of individual plywood boxes in a frame with a common roof. The room boxes are of different depths and unfinished on the back, indicating that the house was intended to be viewed from three sides only.

Rooms in the dollhouse include the front hall, parlor, game room, dining room, red bedroom, music room, upper hallway, white bedroom, green bedroom, kitchen and free-standing tool shed. The tool shed is filled with tiny examples of what one would expect to find in a tool shed, many of which have been handcrafted.

The Parlor of the Morris-Canby-Rumford dollhouse features a peg-wooden doll with tucked-comb hair which dates her from the 1820s and another made more than 100 years later. Of particular interest are the furniture and miniatures which were handcrafted by Samuel Canby Rumford 1939–1940.

In the Red Bedroom we find a doll with a composition head. Because she is unmarked and very similar to miniature dolls made by Ludwig Grenier of Philadelphia, her date of manufacture is estimated to be 1840–1858. She features molded-and-painted wavy hair, delicate painted facial features, and jointed wooden arms and legs.

Fine examples of miniature dolls are found here also. A lovely peg-wooden doll dressed in green gauze and black lace with a painted composition head was the gift of an anonymous donor in 1971.

A handsome male doll with china head, dating from about 1890, is present. One impressive little lady is an early peg-wooden doll, made in Germany about 1810. Her original cost was about one penny! In the kitchen, an unusual black silk doll is found preparing dinner for the family. Fine detail in her construction and costume contribute to her value.

Very little is known about the history of the dollhouse. It was rescued in 1968 from the attic of a Long Island mansion marked for demolition by the contractor. *Doll World* readers are invited to participate in solving the mystery of The Long Island Dollhouse. After looking at the pictures here and in the book or in the Folk Art Center itself, if you have any memory or knowledge of the dollhouse or accessories, please contact Susan Rountree at the Abby Aldrich Rockefeller Folk Art Center, Box 1776, Williamsburg, VA 23187.

Research

Credit for the documented details of individual items in the collection may be attributed

All photos from Dollhouses, Miniature Kitchens and Shops from the Abby Aldrich Rockefeller Folk Art Center by Susan Hight Rountree. Photography by Tom Green; photos courtesy of the Colonial Williamsburg Foundation, Williamsburg, Va.

to the Folk Art Center's curators' dedication to painstaking research.

"Many small items in the kitchens and shops were identified with the help of old toy catalogs. I sat with a group of accessories and paged through catalog after catalog, searching for identical or similar items," Ms. Rountree explained. Photographs of some catalog illustrations are printed in the book, adding reader interest and authenticating dates of items.

Information often comes from unexpected places. At the time of the book's publication, a cubbyhole in the Tile-Roof Kitchen, probably of German origin (1800–1850), was thought to be storage for wood. It struck curators as odd that a storage area would have a door and be located beneath the six-hole stew stove. Later, an illustration in an old catalog became important in identifying the niche as a warming oven.

Archival Storage

Barbara Luck, a curator at the Folk Art Center since 1970, describes state-of-the-art museum storage that protects items in the collection. "Dolls and toys are stored in a 70-degree environment at 55 percent humidity in total darkness. Although some museums separate dolls and accessories that may cause harmful chemical interactions, that may not always be possible when items are extremely old and fragile. Sometimes removing the accessories from contact with the doll may cause more damage than the chemical reaction itself."

Although it is nearly impossible for individual collectors to store precious dolls and accessories under these conditions, there are simple precautions collectors can take to protect their investments. "Store dolls in acid-free tissue paper, in acid-free boxes, away from light sources. Inspect everything regularly to detect any unwelcome 'guests,' use care when cleaning and avoid harsh chemical cleaners," advises Ms. Luck.

Christmas 1996

Christmas 1996 promises to provide another fabulous show. Along with special selections from the collection, visitors may see favorite dolls and miniatures from the collection of noted illustrator Tasha Tudor. Communications associate Sophia Hart invites those who love dolls, dollhouses, miniatures and folk art in general to come prepared to spend a day taking the self-guided tour through the exhibit. "There's a lot to see in a small space!" she warns.

Exhibits and special programs will begin in early November 1996 and continue through February 1997.

If you would like to plan a visit to the Abby Aldrich Rockefeller Folk Art Center at Colonial Williamsburg for this season's spec-

tacular, a vacation planner with event calendar is available free of charge from the public relations office at Colonial Williamsburg. Please call (804) 220–7286 during regular business hours (EST) weekdays. Tell them you read about the exhibit in *Doll World*! **DW**

Thank you to:

Susan Rountree, author of *Dollhouses, Miniature Kitchens and Shops* for sharing her personal insights and unpublished details of the exhibit. Her dedication, research and tireless handwork are appreciated by those unaware of her contribution as well as those who know.

Barbara Luck, assistant curator at the Abby Aldrich Rockefeller Folk Art Center for the kind gift of her time and information about the Center's archiving techniques.

Sophia Hart, communications associate at the Colonial Williamsburg Foundation for background information and for sharing these photographs.

Dollhouses, Miniature Kitchens and Shops may be purchased at gift shops at Colonial Williamsburg or ordered by mail from Colonial Williamsburg, Dept. 023, Box 3532, Williamsburg, VA 23187–3532; (800) 446–9240. The cost is $30.95 (postage paid) by check, money order, Visa, Master-Card, American Express or Discover.

The White Bedroom of the Long Island Dollhouse houses an elegant canopy bed outfitted with a bed covering made from the petticoat of author Susan Rountree's great-grandmother, and a tiny embroidered pillow made from her great-grandfather's handkerchief. An early German peg-wooden doll with carved comb in her hair supervises several diminutive delights, including painted-metal Schoenhut circus figures.

Doll Museums

Coast to Coast

Part 3

By Joyce Rinehart

We conclude our tour of American doll museums in the Central and Eastern states and New England.

Doll museum—just the words light up the eyes of any doll collector. Since few of us have the space or budget to accommodate all the dolls we might like to possess, viewing wonderful one-of-a-kind, extremely old or rare dolls lets us live vicariously. These museums in the Central states, the East and New England contain thousands of such dolls.

Missouri
★ **Society of Memories Doll Museum,** opened 1968. 1115 S. 12th St., St. Joseph, MO 64503, (816) 233–1420. (Located in 1871 church building in Potee Historic District.) Open May–Sept., Tues.–Sun., 1–4 p.m.; closed Oct.–April and Mon. Admission $1.50; children, 50 cents; donations welcome. Seven display rooms; one room is devoted to miniatures, rooms & houses.

Collection: 600 dolls: bisques, chinas, woodens, Schoenhuts, rag dolls, Barbie® dolls, Jumeau, Kestners, Florodora with kid body, Shirley Temple collection including Japanese Shirley, celebrity, fashion, paper dolls, Native American, Raggedy Ann, large French and German dolls, international collections.

Other: Dollhouses, old toys, pedlar samples, wicker carriages and chairs, doll furniture, toy soldiers, bears and vintage costumes.

Pamphlet, postcards and brochure available.

★ **Toy & Miniature Museum of Kansas City,** opened 1982. 5235 Oak St., Kansas City, MO 64112, (816) 333–2055. Open year-round Wed.–Sat., 10 a.m.–4 p.m.; Sun., 1–4 p.m.; closed Mon., Tues., major holidays & two weeks after Labor Day.

Admission $3; seniors & students, $2.50; children, $1.50. 24 rooms, 21,000 square feet; four special exhibits a year. Roger Berg, Jr., administrator.

Collection: 2,500 dolls, 85 percent antique, 15 percent modern: character, Frozen Charlottes & Charlies, Sashas, wax, wax-over-composition, German bisque, bisque theatrical dolls, Golliwog collection, cloth, celebrity, foreign, fashion, paper dolls, puppets, kachina, Native American, Raggedy Ann, Shirley Temple, Barbie dolls.

Other: More than 100 antique dollhouses, extensive collection of miniatures by world's top miniature artisans, doll furniture, buggies, toy soldiers, teddy bears, folk art, farm toys, school toys, churches, boxed toys, Lionel trains.

★ **Bob Kramer's Marionettes & Theater,** opened 1975. 4143 Laclede Ave., St. Louis, MO 63108, (314) 531–3313. Open year-round, 9:30 a.m.–4:30 p.m. Admission to store/exhibit free. Admission to demo/puppet show combo $7; children, $6. Demos 11 a.m. & 1 p.m., shows 11:15 a.m. & 1:15 p.m. 600-square-foot shop & display area.

Collection: More than 800 puppets. Highlights: Puppets from around the world and Bil Baird Marionettes. Seasonal shows and a full-time puppet theater. Puppets for sale.

★ **Eugene Field House & Toy Museum,** opened 1936. 634 S. Broadway, St. Louis, MO 63102, (314) 421–4689. (Located in poet Eugene Field's Victorian house.) Open year-round Wed.–Sat., 10 a.m.–4 p.m.; Sun., 12–4 p.m. Closed Mon., Tues. & national holidays. Open Jan. & Feb. by appointment only. Admission $3; 12–18, $2; 12 & under, 50 cents.

The 1660s Clafin-Richards House is now part of the Wenham Historical Association Museum, Wenham, Mass.

Collection: More than 1,000 dolls displayed in six rooms: antique, modern, cloth, celebrity, foreign, fashion, kachina, Native American, Raggedy Ann, Little Lulu.

Other: Dollhouses, doll furniture, buggies, miniatures, early 1800s and Victorian toy soldiers and bears, toys from early 1800s–1900s, Field family vintage costumes and artifacts. Shop sells dolls.

★ **Annual Kewpiesta Festival,** Branson, Mo., in April. Honors Ozark artist & Kewpie doll creator, Rose O'Neill.

Ohio

★ **Mid-Ohio Historical Museum,** opened May 1984. 700 Winchester Pike, Canal Winchester, OH 43110, (614) 837–5573 (20 minutes from downtown Columbus). Open April–mid-Dec., Wed.–Sat., 11 a.m.–5 p.m. Closed holidays, holiday weekends & mid-Dec.–March. Open Jan.–March by appointment only. Admission $2; under 6, free. 5,000 square feet.

Collection: More than 7,000 dolls, 1700s–modern: wax, Bru Jne, Bru Napoleon, character, wooden, Steiner, Jumeau, Martha Thompson's Ike & Mamie, cloth, foreign, fashion, composition, puppets, Native American, Little Lulu.

Special exhibits: Barbieland, miniature circus, trains, Samantha collection, antique room, Disney collection, celebrity dolls, original Raggedy Ann and Andy (Volland).

Highlights: Schoenhut toy circus, Dionne quints, #1 Barbie doll, GI Joe collection, Star Wars, Shirley Temples, Alice in Wonderland display.

Other: Doll furniture, buggies, toys, miniatures, toy soldiers, bears, doll accessories. Gift shop sells old and new dolls. Doll repair. Annual April doll show/sale.

Wisconsin

★ **Fennimore Doll Museum,** 1140 Lincoln Ave., Fennimore, WI 53809, (608) 822–4100. Collection exhibits are undergoing change. Call to see if they have reopened.

★ **Heirloom Doll Shop, Hospital & Museum,** opened 1984. 416 E. Broadway, Waukesha, WI 52186, (414) 544–4739. Open year-round Mon.–Sat.; closed Sun. & major holidays. Admission free. William Zito, owner.

Collection: 2,000 antique and modern dolls: cloth, celebrity, foreign, fashion, puppets, Raggedy Ann, Shirley Temple, Little Lulu.

Highlights: Antiques, mint-in-box collectibles and Barbie dolls. Shop has more than 300 antique and collectible dolls for sale.

The East

New Jersey

★ **Doll Castle Doll Museum,** opened June 1983. 37 Belvidere Ave., Washington, NJ 07882, (908) 689–7042. Open summer months by appointment only. Admission $2.50; children, $1.

Collection: More than 2,000 antique and modern dolls displayed in four rooms on second floor of Mueller Building. Collection of Edwina Mueller ("81 years young") of *Doll Castle News.* Cloth, celebrity, foreign, fashion, paper dolls, puppets, kachina, totem pole, Native American, Raggedy Ann, Shirley Temple, Little Lulu, original artists' dolls, 200 Barbie dolls.

Highlights: Clown by Emmet Kelly, 100-year-old dollhouse completely furnished, real-fur bear.

Other: Dollhouses, doll furniture, buggies, toys, miniatures, bears, doll-related items. Shop, postcards, brochure. (See *Doll World*, June 1994, for article and photos.)

★ **Good Fairy Doll Museum & Hospital,** opened 1967. 205 Walnut Ave., Cranford, NJ 07616, (908) 276–3815 (Exit 137 Garden State Parkway, five lights, then left. No sign on building.) Open by appointment only. Admission $1.25. Mom-and-pop–style museum of three rooms. Elizabeth Connors, owner.

An unmarked German doll, a very old French Jumeau and a K★R Simon & Halbig are on display at the Society of Memories Doll Museum, St. Joseph, Mo.

Collection: Modern dolls, foreign, fashion, puppets, kachina, small totem poles, Native American, comic characters, 25 Indian chiefs, monks, nuns, rabbis, Ginny and other Vogue dolls, carnival dolls, black history dolls, Kewpies, parians, Disney collectibles, life-size wax dolls.

Highlights: Dionnes, bronze knight, mission dolls, Rip Van Winkle and 10 poet dolls by doll artist Nuby; Greek, Syrian.

Other: Maccabee Bible, player piano, Indian chief's warbonnet with beaded cross, dollhouses, toy soldiers, miniatures, animated toys, iron banks, bears, sports collectibles, mouse house. Dolls for sale, postcards, brochure.

Mid-Ohio Historical Museum, Canal Winchester, Ohio, is proud to display this 38" Bru Jne from 1880s.

Photo courtesy of Mid-Ohio Historical Museum.

New York

★ **The Museum at Stony Brook,** opened 1939. 1208 Rte. 25-A, Stony Brook, NY 11790, (516) 751–0066. Open year-round Wed.–Fri., 9 a.m.–4:30 p.m.; closed Sat., Sun. & holidays. Admission $6; seniors, $4; children, $3.

Collection: 250 dolls: antique, modern, cloth, celebrity, foreign, fashion, paper dolls, puppets, Raggedy Ann, Shirley Temple.

Other: 11 dollhouses, doll furniture, buggies, toys, miniatures, toy soldiers, bears, vintage costumes, wing of miniature rooms, 12 buildings with world-renowned carriage collection, art collection.

★ **National Museum of the American Indian.** 3401 Bruckner Blvd., Bronx; NY 10461, (718) 430–6846. (A branch of the Smith-sonian Institution.) Open 10 a.m.–5 p.m. every day but Christmas. Admission free.

Collection: "Several thousand dolls from Aztec to Zuni" including 700 Hopi kachina dolls, 60 Iroquois cornhusk dolls. They are not displayed as a collection but kept with their respective cultural groups. Only a few dolls are on display; most are in storage. Dolls are being prepared for move to Washington, D.C., which will take several years.

★ **The Strong Museum,** opened 1982. 1 Manhattan Square, Rochester, NY 14607, (716) 263–2700. Open Mon.–Sat., 10 a.m.–5 p.m.; Sun., 1–5 p.m.; closed Christmas Day, New Year's Day, July 4th and Thanksgiving Day. Admission $5; seniors & students, $4; children, $3.

Collection: 20,000 dolls, 60 percent antique, 40 percent modern: cloth, celebrity, foreign, fashion, paper dolls, puppets, kachina, Native American, Raggedy Ann, Shirley Temple, black dolls.

Other: Dollhouses, doll furniture, buggies, toys, miniatures, toy soldiers, bears, vintage costumes. "More than half a million objects." Shop sells dolls. Café, library.

★ **Victorian Doll Museum Chili Doll Hospital,** opened 1970. 4332 Buffalo Road, North Chili, NY 14515, (716) 247–0130 (20 minutes west of downtown Rochester; barn-red, two-story building just past Roberta Wesleyan College.) Open Feb.–Dec., Tues.–Sat., 10 a.m.–4 p.m.; closed Sun., Mon., Jan. & major holidays. Admission $2; children, $1. Three rooms of exhibits, shop & doll hospital. Linda Greenfield, owner, started collecting at age 8.

Collection: 2,000 dolls, 60 percent antique, 40 percent modern: bisque, china, wood, wax, metal, felt, ivory, papier-mâché, Kewpie, paper dolls, Schoenhut dolls and circus, celebrity, fashion, advertising, Alexander, Effanbee, Ginny, Norah Wellings, Lenci, Frozen Charlottes, celluloids, foreign, Queen Elizabeth and other paper dolls, puppets, kachina, Native American, Raggedy Ann, Shirley Temple, 1950s composition.

Other: Noah's ark, toys, action puppet theater, dollhouses, doll furniture, buggies, toys, miniatures. Special displays: Dolls of Rochester resident and artist Eloise Wilkins. Doll repairs, appraisals. Shop sells old and new dolls, doll books and magazines.

Pennsylvania

★ **Mary Merritt Doll Museum,** opened 1963. R.D. 2, Douglassville, PA 19518, (610) 385–3809. (Located on Rte. 422 between Pottstown & Reading.) Open year-round Mon.–Sat., 10 a.m.–5 p.m.; Sun., 1–5 p.m. Closed holidays. Admission $3; seniors, $2.50; children, $1.50, 5 & under, free. Includes admission to Childhood Museum next door. Marjorie Merritt Darrah, curator.

Collection: 3,500 antique dolls collected by Robert and Mary Merritt: Seventh century Egyptian bone doll, Queen Anne woodens, milliners, pedlar, Joel Ellis, Greiner, wax, Pumpkin Heads, bonnet dolls, china, parian, French fashion, bisque, Frozen Charlottes and Charlies, German jointed, Schoenhut, rag dolls, foreign, mechanicals, paper dolls, papier-mâché, 1930s Shirley Temples.

Other: 40 furnished miniature rooms and dollhouses, 75-piece Schoenhut circus, Schoenhut safari set, extensive collection of French mechanical dolls, engines, carriages, Noah's arks, lead soldiers, hobby horses, doll dishes, a full-size replica of an 1850 Philadelphia toy shop. Gift shop sells antique and collectible dolls, doll clothing and accessories, pamphlet, brochure, book, postcards.

★ **Mary Stolz Doll Shop & Museum,** opened 1986. McCole Rd. (R.D. 6, Box 6767), East Stroudsburg, PA 18301, (717) 588–7566. (Located off Rte. 209 near Bushkill, directly across from Pocono Indian Museum.) Open year-round Mon.–Sun., 10:30 a.m.–5:30

p.m. Admission $2.50; seniors, $2.25; children, $1.25; 3 & under, free. Jan Stolz, owner.

Collection: 125 dolls displayed in three rooms, 50 percent antique, 50 percent modern: cloth, foreign, fashion, puppets, Raggedy Ann, Shirley Temple, artists dolls.

Other: Dollhouses, toys, miniature rooms, bears. Modern display of bears and dolls. Hobby Hut upstairs displays trains, planes, models. Shop sells dolls, dollhouses, miniatures.

New England

Connecticut

★ **New Britain Youth Museum,** founded 1956. 30 High St., New Britain, CT 06051, (203) 225–3020. Open year-round Tues.–Sat., 1–5 p.m., closed Sun. & Mon. Admission free/donation.

Collection: 500 dolls displayed in two rooms, 10 percent antique, 80 percent modern: cloth, foreign, puppets, kachina and German bisque.

Highlights: Circus, Native American dolls. Notable rotating exhibits: American folk dolls, 100 years of commercial dolls, and dolls of Japan.

Other: Dollhouses, doll furniture, miniatures, toys, original children's books illustrations. Museum shop sells doll postcards.

Maine

★ **Portland Museum of Art,** founded 1882. 7 Congress Square, Portland, ME 04101, (207) 775–6148. Open year-round Tues.–Sat., 10 a.m.–5 p.m.; Sun., 12–5 p.m. Admission $6; seniors & students, $5; children, $1.

Collection: Primarily an art museum with a notable collection of Winslow Homer watercolors. They have about a dozen hand-colored American paper dolls from the mid-1800s, plus a 1920s Cuban black Mammy doll, German bisque and French wax-head and china-head Jenny Lind dolls of mid-1800s. Call ahead if you wish to see the dolls or paper dolls, as they are currently in storage. Museum shop has dolls for sale.

Massachussetts

★ **The Children's Museum.** 300 Congress St., Boston, MA 02210-1034, (617) 426–8855. Open year-round, summer daily, 10 a.m.–5 p.m., Fri. till 9 p.m. Closed Mon., Thanksgiving, Christmas, New Year's Day. Admission $7; seniors & children 2–15, $6.

Collection: Dolls, dollhouses, games, toys. Gift shop has paper dolls and excellent selection of children's books.

★ **Yesteryears Doll Museum,** founded 1961. 143 Main St., Sandwich, MA 02563, (508) 888–1711. 2 floors of 1833 large white church with red trim at corner of Main and River sts. Open mid-May–end of Oct., Mon.–Sat., 10 a.m.–4 p.m. Admission $3; seniors, $2.50; children, $1.50.

Collection: "Several thousand" dolls, 75 percent antique, 25 percent modern: cloth, celebrity, foreign, fashion, paper dolls, puppets, kachina, Oriental, Raggedy Ann, Shirley Temple, Native American, Disney, collection of Madame Alexander and modern artists' dolls.

Other: Dollhouses, doll furniture, buggies, strollers, toys, miniatures, toy soldiers, bears.

Notable: Nuremberg kitchen, milliners, confectioners and toy shops. Special exhibits: Disneyana, Toys and Tales (books with their corresponding dolls and toys). Museum shop "one-stop doll shopping." Repair, restoration, appraisals and study group.

Cinderella at the Ball and dolls in Louis XIV period costumes were designed by artist Nuby for the Good Fairy Doll Museum, Cranford, N.J.

★ **Wenham Museum,** founded 1921, Doll wing opened 1952. 132 Main St., Wenham, MA 01984, (508) 468–2377. Open year-round Mon.–Fri., 11 a.m.–4 p.m.; Sat., 1–4 p.m.; Sun. 2–5 p.m. Closed all major holidays. Admission $3; seniors, $2.50; children, $1. Displayed in an addition to the 1664 Claflin-Richards House. "World-renowned" collection.

Collection: 5,000 dolls and toys in six changing exhibits each year, 95 percent antique, 5 percent modern: cloth, celebrity, foreign, fashion, paper dolls, puppets, kachina, Raggedy Ann, Shirley Temple, Little Lulu, Native American, wax, papier-mâché, wood, bisque.

Other: Dollhouses, doll furniture, buggies, dishes, tea sets, toy soldiers, miniatures, bears, vintage costumes. Has excellent collection of paper dolls, costumes and toy cutouts which they will show to visitors on request. Museum shop, pamphlet, postcards, brochure, classes, Collectors Days lectures/workshops.

Rhode Island

★ **The Doll Museum,** opened 1987. 520 Thames St., Newport, RI 02840, (401) 847–0405. Open year-round Mon., Wed.–Sat., 10 a.m.–5 p.m.; Sun., 12–5 p.m.; closed Tues. Museum owner Linda Edward, "doll addict." Admission $2; seniors, $1.50; children, $1. Group 50 percent discount with prior notice.

Collection: About 700 dolls: cloth, celebrity, foreign, fashion, paper dolls, kachina, Raggedy Ann, Shirley Temple, Native American, modern artists. Special exhibits twice a year, changing topics.

Other: Dollhouses, doll furniture, buggies, strollers, toys, miniatures, toy soldiers. Museum shop sells dolls, books, postcards. Slide presentation with lecture for groups.

We've covered only a smattering of the doll museums scattered coast to coast. They frequently open, close, move or put collections in storage, so it's prudent to call before journeying long distances to visit one.

As you travel, look in phone books under "historical society museums," "children's museums" and "doll" or "toy" museums. Call any doll shop listed and inquire about local or nearby museums. Stop at state tourist information centers. Some states, such as Oklahoma, have prepared a brochure describing all the museums in their state. Auto club tour guides also list many museums. You're sure to discover new places to see, buy and enjoy dolls. **DW**

Czech Puppets Make Worldwide Debut

Zdenka Cerna washing plaster of paris doll heads.

By Jacqueline Ruyak

Dating to medieval times, modern puppeteers keep Czech tradition alive with production and traveling shows.

After one of several recent visits to the former Czechoslovakia (on January 1, 1993, Czechoslovakia separated into the independent Czech and Slovak Republics), I brought home several of the handmade puppets which had charmed me on each visit there. My mother took one look at them and demanded, "Why haven't you brought these back before? They're wonderful! And they'd make great gifts!" The story ends, of course, with the puppets gracing a wall of my mother's Pennsylvania farmhouse.

Those particular puppets were made by Rezek, the best of the commercial puppet makers now in the Czech Republic. Paul Rezek, who founded this company several years ago, is simply a fan of puppets and old-time puppet theater.

Tradition

Puppet plays are among the oldest forms of theater in the former Czechoslovakia, going back to the mystery plays of medieval times. Until World War II, says Vladimir Sindler,

the general manager at Rezek, almost every village in Czechoslovakia had a small puppet theater, and many families had their own puppets, often handmade.

Books of puppet plays for home performances were perennial best sellers throughout the country. Among the always-popular plays were those based on fairy tales, such as *Little Red Riding Hood*, and classics such as *Hamlet* and *Faust*.

Nowadays, however, people find their entertainment on television and most people no longer know how to manipulate the marionettes that once provided home amusement. But even today, says Sindler, Czech and Slovak families are likely to attend a puppet performance at least once a year.

Traveling groups still perform in villages, and there are still about 15 puppet theaters in the Czech and Slovak republics. There are four such groups in Prague alone, but like most contemporary puppet groups, they use large-scale puppets and have incorporated actors into their performances.

Between World Wars I and II, there were many small companies making puppets in Czechoslovakia, but they disappeared when a communist regime took control of the country in 1948. Twelve years ago, however, Pavl Rezek decided to start making and marketing the marionettes that he had loved from his youth, and he formed the company that now bears his name.

Rezek Puppets

Rezek now makes about 40 marionette models. Among the more popular are harlequins and Pierrots, devils, witches, clowns, fools, princes and princesses. The puppets are about 10" long and their bodies are usually made of oak.

The company produces about 20,000 puppets a year. Much of the work, which is compartmentalized, is done in small apartments in Prague or its suburbs.

The narrow, suburban apartment where Zdenka Cerna and two colleagues paint heads is typical. The heads are made of plaster of paris mixed to a special Rezek formula. Some of the molds used to make the heads date back to the 1870s; others have been created for more contemporary puppet characters.

Painting

After receiving the "raw" heads which are made elsewhere, Cerna removes any burrs or imperfections, then washes the heads and dries them. Using latex paints and tempera, she then paints them. She covers the head with a white base coat, then paints in the face and hair and shades in the cheeks and chin.

Last and most crucial are the eyes, which, Sindler points out, must be exaggerated rather than natural. Cerna, who only recently started painting heads, concurs as she critically examines one of the many finished batches of heads stacked on the shelves that line the studio walls.

The 20 people who work at Rezek have diverse backgrounds. The hardworking, energetic Sindler, for example, is a former telecommunications engineer. Six-year veteran Ivana Poppova, now one of the stars of the Rezek work force, used to be a secretary. Now, however, Poppova works at home in her spotless Prague apartment, making costumes for the puppets which she also assembles, clothes and finishes.

Assembly

To assemble a puppet, Poppova first wires the arms and legs to the trunk. She then dresses the puppet in the costume she has made for it. Taking obvious enjoyment in her work, Poppova next attaches the head, which is then attached to the crossbar used for manipulating the marionette.

Poppova then threads the strings which link the puppet's limbs to the crossbar, starting with the legs. Those done, she hangs the puppet up and loops the strings onto its hands. A quick adjustment in balance and the puppet is done. Watching Poppova at work, it's easy to understand why the general manager had introduced her as "the best."

Quality

The company's success has spawned imitators, many of whom gained their hands-on experience working at Rezek. On my last visit to Prague, the city seemed to be flooded with puppets—from the garishly kitsch to the artistic one-of-a-kind.

Of the commercially marketed puppets, though, those made by Rezek stand out. And to make sure that customers know what they are getting, in 1992 the company created a simple, distinctive logo—the name Rezek printed in a bold, black script on a dark yellow background—for its expanding line of puppets.

As another step in quality control, Rezek is now looking for shop sites in Prague and elsewhere in the Czech Republic in order to market its puppets directly. No matter how or where its products are sold, though, Rezek remains committed to making quality marionettes.

As the Czech Republic makes the hard transition to a market economy, puppets remain luxury goods beyond the reach of the average Czech. The people at Rezek look forward to the day when their puppets will be as popular with Czechs as they are proving to be with people abroad.

For more information, contact Vladimir Sindler, Fa. Rezek, Vrsovická 83, 10500 Prague 10, Czech Republic. **DW**

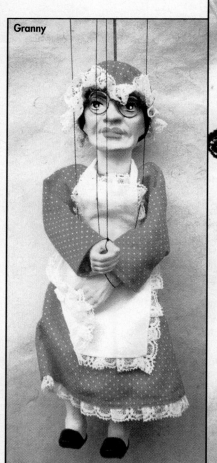

Granny

Witch

Pierrot

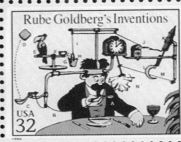

"Strippers" of the Doll Kingdom

Part 1

By Jane Carlton

The funnies became part of newspapers in 1895 or '96. Soon after, manufacturers capitalized on their popularity and favorite characters came to life as dolls.

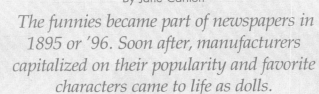

"Our people don't want their wit on a separate dish … it must come in daily with our coffee," proclaimed a 19th century newspaper reader. In October 1995, the United States Post Office celebrated "getting our wit with our coffee" by issuing comic commemorative stamps. *Doll World* is commemorating that centennial (which some say actually dates from 1896) with a series of articles on dolls which debuted in the comics.

Comics as Dolls

You may be surprised to learn that some of your favorite conventional dolls began their lives as "strippers." Raggedy Ann and Andy, Campbell Kids (these googly-eye dolls are often displayed with matching feeding dishes), the Gibson Girl, teddy bears and even Uncle Sam are fine examples. They have been produced by the most unpretentious manufacturers from the crudest of materials. Raggedy Ann and Andy are often, appropriately, rag.

The most sophisticated manufacturers have produced comic dolls from the finest materials. Simon & Halbig produced a bisque Uncle Sam in the 1890s. Kewpies range from cheap (at the time) celluloid carnival prizes to fine bisque figurines.

Even Madame Alexander stooped to producing Brenda Starr. Whole corporations owe their existence to comic dolls. Would the Mego Company even exist without comic superheroes? I doubt it.

Often comic character dolls literally lunge from their pages. Pull their jumping-jack strings and they do the splits; squeeze them and they squeak; put batteries in them and they bump and grind; wind them up and they play a tune. Since it is so hard to draw a line between real dolls, action toys, figurines, stuffed animals and puppets, I've included each in this series.

First Merchandise Connection
The first recognized U.S. comic strip character to spin off into advertising buttons, cracker boxes, cigarettes, fans, a Broadway play and, yes, even dolls, was the Yellow Kid by R.F. Outcault.

This urchin's nightshirt was blue or red, sometimes dotted in Outcault's early *Hogan's Alley* comic strip, before a printer, Charles Salzberg, experimenting with new inks, dyed his shirt yellow. From then on, the name of the kid and the comic strip matched the unplanned conception. (The battle between publishers Hearst and Pulitzer over the right to use the *Yellow Kid* comic strip gave us the expression "yellow journalism.") The first Yellow Kid doll, made in 1897 of hand-painted plaster of paris, is now a treasure.

Though the comics originally lived up to their vernacular name "the funnies," they soon diverged to include cutesy kiddy stories, serial dramas, talking animals, action heroes, ghosts and goblins and even erotica, with corresponding dolls representing every category. They have provided propaganda during war with corresponding dolls to rally around (Uncle Sam, for example); they've incited readers to vote for a specific candidate ("Teddy Bear Roosevelt") and buy products (Li'l Abner represented Cream of Wheat).

Paper Dolls & Beyond
Some evolved into paper dolls; others originated as paper dolls. Many spun off to become comic book characters. Others, such as Dick Tracy, moved up to radio, television and movies.

Shoot-'em-up star William Boyd's alter ego, Hopalong Cassidy, began as the figment of an artist's imagination; Hollywood had to hunt for a human Hopalong who matched the comic creation. And the curvaceous, pugnacious, three-dimensional Jane Fonda wasn't the first Barbarella; the original was flat as paper—fashioned by French cartoonist Claude Forest.

American comics have been exported as freely as Coca-Cola, sometimes with their original names, often with an alias. So, if you run into a doll which is a dead ringer for Blondie (reputedly the most widely read strip internationally) wearing a tag that reads

"Pepila," don't pass her up. That's her Latinized name. Dagwood may be Dagobert, Emile or Lorenzo.

But Americans don't hold the patent on comic strips and their matching dolls. "The whole world lieth in the witty one." One of my most interesting "strippers" came from Japan and is labeled in undecipherable script.

Mint-in-Box
At the risk of angering some collectors, I must admit that the expression mint-in-box makes me sad. It doesn't bother me for a kid to care for a doll well enough for it to be in excellent condition years later. But MIB indicates that the giver of the gift reserved the right to keep the kid from playing with it. However, as with other collectible dolls, age, rarity and condition affect their price.

If you find an old one in its original box, expect it to be *at least* 25 percent higher than its twin without the coffin. In fact, an *empty box* from Li'l Abner and his Dogpatch Band is listed in a toy price guide at $22–$44.

Because comic dolls are derivative works in which another person's art is "recast, transformed or adapted," rather than bearing a trademark, they are usually marked with "copyright" or © and a date.

And, yes this *is art*. When I compare the talent required to create the expression on the face of DaVinci's *Mona Lisa* with Fred Lasswell's Lowizie Smif (original spelling), or the entwinement of characters in Rodin's *The Kiss* with Chic Young's Dagwood fighting Herb Woodley, the cartoonist wins, especially when I consider that he creates a new strip seven days a week, putting in his characters' mouths terse words that rival Mark Twain's for wit.

When Was It Made?
Though it is possible that a doll was actually created after the copyright date, it is certain that it wasn't made before it. If you are considering reproducing characters still covered by the copyright, be sure to obtain permission from any cartoonist, publisher, syndicate or movie producer involved.

If a doll has lost its tag, the materials used in its manufacture may help you deduce its age. Celluloid and composition went out of style with the end of World War II, being replaced by hard plastic. Numerous painted tin action dolls were made in occupied Japan after World War II. Magic Skin (popular only during World War II) and rubber were replaced by soft vinyl in the early 1950s.

Saran hair that grew right out of a doll's scalp began to replace wigs in the early 1950s. Though dolls and animals are still made of cloth, the fibers in those fabrics and their stuffing may help you establish the date of manufacture.

When bears were stuffed with sawdust or cotton, their labels never touted their washableness. No-iron doll dresses showed up about 1956, replacing rayon and cotton. About that time, plastic shoes succeeded cloth with cardboard soles. Although wire-limbed flexies have been around since the late 1930s, it wasn't till the early '50s that foam-rubber–covered bendies came along, soon giving way to pliable vinyl.

Resources
Since it is rare for a comic strip character doll to predate its original strip, you may begin your search for their pedigrees in *Horn's Encyclopedia of Comics* or *American Comic Strip Classics* available from the United States Postal Service, (800) STAMP24, for $34.15 with 40 stamps thrown in for free. Though doll price guides occasionally go slumming in laugh-land, you are more likely to locate comic dolls in toy price guides.

Future articles in this series will cover funny families, liberated ladies, urchins and orphans, cowboys and Indians, cops and robbers, superheroes, bachelors from Milquetoast to Macho, animals and Disneyana. **DW**

Make Your Own Greeting Cards

By Bonnie Boots

Let your favorite dolls send greetings to family and friends on those "oh, so special" days!

People who make and collect dolls often enjoy decorating their homes with seasonal displays. If you spend time bringing your dolls to life by arranging little scenes with them, there's a way you can share these with family and friends. Take photographs and make them into greeting cards! It's easy and inexpensive, and the joy it brings will last for years.

Every year I make my own Christmas cards featuring a comical doll. I have great fun imagining the situations I can put this character into each year, and my friends always get a laugh when they receive my cards. This is one greeting that is not thrown away after the holidays!

I have friends who take photographs of their dolls and make them into postcards, using them for correspondence all year long. It's a great way to share their treasures with others. Whether you use dolls you've made or dolls you've collected, you will enjoy planning and making your own greeting cards.

You probably already have all the tools and equipment you need. Basically, all you will need are a 35mm camera, a roll of ASA 100 color film, something to reflect light (a wall mirror, a sheet of white tag board or a piece of cardboard covered with crumpled aluminum foil), a table to set up your display, a backdrop (2 yards of a solid-color fabric or photographer's backdrop paper, available at many camera supply stores), and an area inside your home where a window admits a good amount of daylight.

Choose a Location

First, decide where in your home you will be taking your photos. You need a big window that will admit a lot of daylight, perhaps a living room picture window or big dining room windows. It is best if you can use the window in a room with white or light-colored walls, as these will not reflect color onto your display. If you must use a room with deeply colored walls, you may want to tack up a white sheet around the area.

Watch the window you choose and examine how the light changes throughout the day. You want a good amount of

A simple background often shows off the doll best.

light to illuminate the scene, but it is best if this is soft light. Taking a photo in full sunlight in the summer may result in glaring highlights and hard shadows in your finished picture. You may find that the light is softer and more flattering early in the morning or on an overcast day. Though I always take my photos in front of the same window, I take them at different times of the day depending on the season.

Set the Scene

Once you have chosen an area and decided when the light is best, set up your scene. First decide what sort of greeting card you will be making. If it is going to be an all-occasion card, you can set up any sort of tableau with your dolls. A display of your favorite dolls having a tea party could be charming, or you

Cards courtesy of Bonnie Boots.

Plastic pink flamingos add the perfect Florida touch to this whimsical card.

might want to show off just one special doll. If you will be making greeting cards for a particular holiday, you can really let your imagination get to work!

Just imagine what fun you can have setting up tableaus for Halloween or Valentine's Day. Perhaps you have some white bisque Cupid dolls that could be posed standing alongside a big red heart that says "You're a real doll! I love you!"

For Halloween, it would be exciting to pose a doll next to a miniature pumpkin or alongside a spooky-looking twig draped with spiderweb floss. For the Fourth of July you could outfit a few of your favorite dolls with flags and arrange them in a parade.

Perhaps the most enjoyable card to plan is your own Christmas card. Designing this card yourself really makes it a very special greeting. Be sure to plan this card well in advance of the holidays, as you'll want it to be absolutely perfect. I usually decide on the theme for my card sometime in August, so I have plenty of time to make the doll and take a good photo. Sometimes I shoot this picture two or three times to get it just right.

Christmas Card

In the Christmas card I shot for 1995, I had a crazy old lady in fuzzy slippers and a housecoat dressing up her lawn flamingos with a wreath and Christmas lights. The first time I shot the picture, I had her on a brick patio with a stucco wall behind her, standing next to a miniature palm tree. It looked great to my eyes, but when I got the film developed I was very disappointed. There were so many things crowding the picture that my doll was lost in the confusion.

I reshot the picture against a solid yellow background with nothing in the scene except the doll and her flamingos. I put one little sprig of air plant near the doll to indicate she was in her yard. That simple scene made a much better picture.

Arrange for the Shot

When you have chosen a scene, it's time to get ready and actually shoot the picture. Set up a table near the window you have chosen and arrange it so that the light from the window will strike your doll display from the side, rather than from the back.

Continued on page 53

Girl of the
LIMBERLOST

*Introduce a youngster to Gene Stratton-Porter's popular novels or remember
a friend who shares fond memories of these books by creating this doll inspired
by the author's best-selling novel. Present it as a gift with a copy of the book;
both are sure to become treasured possessions.*

Shortly after the turn of the century, Doubleday published a book written by a middle-aged woman from Geneva, a small rural community in northeastern Indiana. It soon captured the hearts of millions of readers and became a best-selling novel. Her fourth book, *A Girl of the Limberlost,* was the first of Gene Stratton-Porter's five best-selling novels, each selling over a million copies—more than any other best-selling author from 1895–1945.

Although marketed as popular romance, Gene Stratton-Porter described her novels as slender threads of romance on which she had strung "every gem from nature their weight would bear." It was her intention in writing these books to lead afield every individual she could influence, "but with such reverence instilled in his touch, that devastation would not be complete."

The setting for her early novels was the nearby Limberlost, an extensive wetland slowly being drained during the 24 years of her residence there. She entangled the natural beauty that she found within the Limberlost around the lives of characters inspired by individuals with whom she came in daily contact—simple, moral folk. Gene Stratton-Porter guaranteed the natural history in these books to be true to her working grounds, and they remain today far more than popular romance. They are valuable historic documentation of the era.

Born Aug. 17, 1863, Gene Stratton-Porter was farsighted in her views of conservation, a fact attested to by the relevance for today's readers of environmental issues addressed in her books more than 90 years ago—providing a glimpse into the past, and inspiration for the future.

Julie Munson's Girl of the Limberlost doll is offered here in commemoration of the 133rd anniversary of Gene Stratton-Porter's birth.

—Marla Freeman
Reprint editions of Gene Stratton-Porter's books are available from Limberlost State Historic Site, P.O. Box 356, Geneva, IN 46740, (219) 368–7428. Proceeds return to the site.

Girl of the Limberlost Doll & Costume

by Julie Munson

Materials
- 1 yard 45"-wide muslin (for doll and pinafore)
- ½ yard solid-color fabric (for pantaloons)
- ½ yard calico fabric (for dress and hair bow)
- Polyester fiberfill
- Sewing needle and thread
- 2 (½") 2-hole black buttons (for eyes)
- Small amount black embroidery floss
- Long sculpting needle
- Acrylic paint: black, white and red
- #10/0 paintbrush
- #6 paintbrush
- Craft glue
- Powdered blusher
- Blue powdered eye shadow
- 1¾ yards ¾"-wide cotton lace (for dress)
- 1 yard ⅜"-wide cotton lace (for pinafore)
- 1 pair cotton infant's socks to match fabric
- 1 (60-yard) skein rug and craft yarn (for hair)
- 4 (³⁄₁₆") buttons
- Dried flowers or herbs
- Small bird

Pattern notes
Please read directions before beginning.
Pantaloon pattern piece is reduced. Enlarge this pattern piece using a copy machine as noted on the pattern.
Make ¼" seams unless otherwise stated.
To make working with yarn for hair easier, roll skein into ball before beginning.

Body
1. From muslin, cut two body pieces on fold, four arms, four legs and one nose.
2. Sew body pieces together, leaving open as indicated for stuffing. Sew two arm pieces and two leg pieces together,

leaving open as indicated for stuffing. Repeat for remaining arm and leg pieces. Trim seams to ⅛".
3. Turn pieces; stuff firmly to within ½" of openings. Turn opening edges under ¼"; whipstitch closed. Hand-stitch around each arm approximately 5" from top; pull stitching to gather and secure firmly.
4. Make a running stitch at top of arms; attach arms to body at shoulders. Whipstitch legs to bottom of body.

Face
1. Mark placement for eyes above cheek area 1" apart. With doll-sculpting needle, bring black embroidery floss from back of head to placement of one eye, leaving length of floss for tying. Thread button onto floss; bring needle back through head from placement point to back. Pull tightly to sculpt cheek slightly; tie floss at back of head. Repeat for second eye.
2. Make running stitch around nose ⅛" from edge; gather slightly. Roll a small amount of stuffing and insert in nose; pull thread tightly and fasten securely. Trim ravelings.
3. Apply a small amount of craft glue to back of nose; place on face just below and between eyes, holding in place with pins until dry.
4. For mouth, dip blunt end of #10/0 paintbrush into red paint; make three small dots in shape of heart below nose. With brush end, fill in heart shape with red paint, pulling a fine line up and out on each side of mouth for a smile. Highlight lower lip with a dab of white paint.
5. Paint eyebrows and eyelashes with black paint and #10/0 paintbrush.
6. Let face dry completely. Apply powdered blusher to cheeks, nose and chin. Apply powdered blue eye shadow lightly over eyes.

Clothing
1. With black paint and #10/0 paintbrush, paint shoes to paint line indicated on pattern. When dry, use #6 paintbrush and white paint to paint scallops. Make a white dot in each scallop for button.
2. Cut two pantaloons on fold from solid-color fabric. Sew crotch seam on each piece; trim to ⅛". Turn one piece right side out; leave second piece wrong side out. Place right-side-out piece inside other piece, matching raw edges. Sew inner leg seam from bottom of leg to bottom of leg. Turn right side out.
3. Double-fold calico fabric so there is one lengthwise fold and one crosswise fold. Place dress pattern on fabric so front fold is on crosswise fold and top fold is on lengthwise fold (Fig. 1). Cut one; cut hair

bow as shown in diagram. Cut out neck opening.
4. With right sides together, sew underarm/side seams. Make ¼" bottom hem. Sew one piece of ¾"-wide lace over hemstitching; sew second piece of ¾"-wide lace above it so pieces slightly overlap.
5. For pinafore, cut one bodice front on fold, two bodice backs and one 6" x 30" piece for skirt from muslin. Sew shoulder seams and side seams of bodice. Make ¼" hem on one long edge of skirt. Gather remaining long edge of skirt to fit bodice. Sew skirt to bodice. Hem bodice back opening ¼". Sew ⅜"-wide lace over hemstitching at bottom of skirt. Turn bodice neckline under ¼"; sew remaining ⅜"-wide lace around neckline. Sew four ³⁄₁₆" buttons down center front of pinafore bodice.
6. Cut ribbing section off infant's socks for stockings.

Dressing
1. Place pantaloons on doll. Turn top under ¼"; make running stitch around top, beginning and ending at back. Pull stitches to gather; secure thread. Turn leg edges under and gather in same manner.
2. Pull sock ribbing over painted shoes and tuck under pantaloons.
3. Place dress on doll. Turn neck and sleeve edges under ¼"; stitch and gather as for pantaloons. Glue piece of ¾"-wide lace over neck gathers.
4. Place pinafore on doll, overlapping bodice opening in back; whipstitch closed.

Hair
1. Fold 6-foot length of yarn in half. Beginning at back left side of head, attach yarn with thread in 5" loops across base of scalp to right side, cut yarn. Make four more rows of hair in this manner across back of head.
2. Working in same manner, attach yarn around top front of head, just over seam line, making loops 6"–7".
3. Cut loops of hair. Pull front and sides of hair into a ponytail (Fig. 2), making sure head is covered. Secure ponytail with thread. Lift section up; drizzle craft glue over head. Arrange hair and secure in place with pins until dry.
4. In same manner, attach 1½"–2" loops of yarn across front of head for bangs. Cut loops.
5. Trim ends evenly. Tie strip of calico fabric in hair for bow.

Finishing
1. Stitch ends of hands together as shown in photo.
2. Glue dried flowers in hands. Glue small bird on shoulder. **DW**

Girl of the Limberlost Pattern Pieces

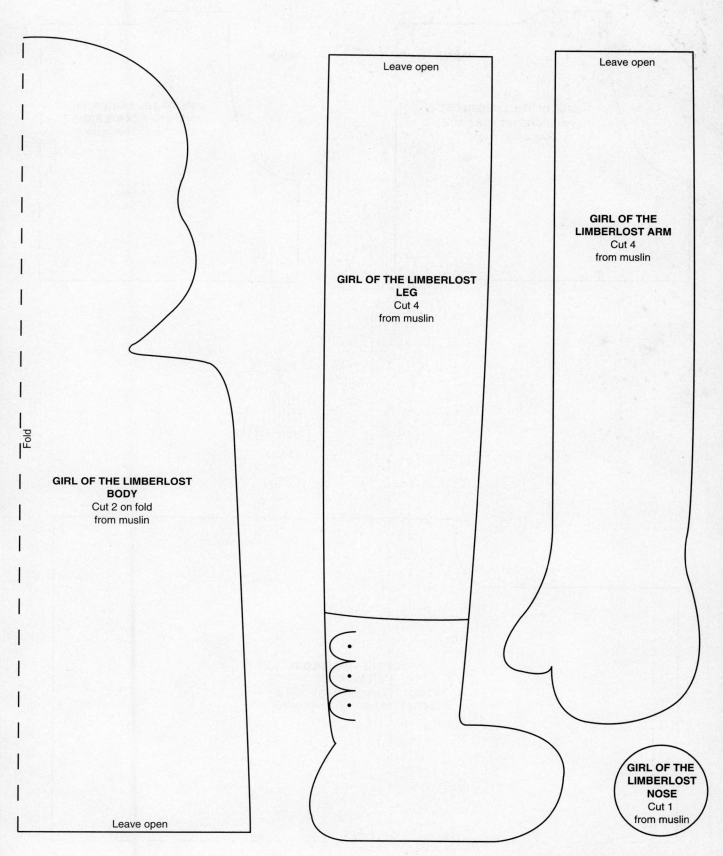

Leave open

GIRL OF THE
LIMBERLOST ARM
Cut 4
from muslin

GIRL OF THE LIMBERLOST
LEG
Cut 4
from muslin

Fold

GIRL OF THE LIMBERLOST
BODY
Cut 2 on fold
from muslin

Leave open

GIRL OF THE
LIMBERLOST
NOSE
Cut 1
from muslin

Girl of the Limberlost Pattern Pieces

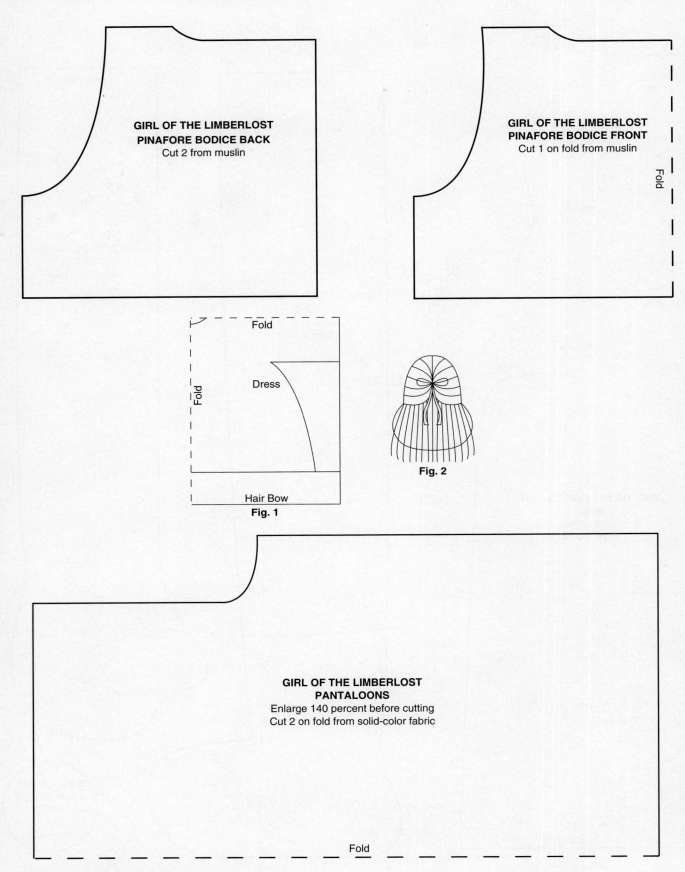

**GIRL OF THE LIMBERLOST
PINAFORE BODICE BACK**
Cut 2 from muslin

**GIRL OF THE LIMBERLOST
PINAFORE BODICE FRONT**
Cut 1 on fold from muslin

Fold

Fold

Fold

Dress

Hair Bow
Fig. 1

Fig. 2

**GIRL OF THE LIMBERLOST
PANTALOONS**
Enlarge 140 percent before cutting
Cut 2 on fold from solid-color fabric

Fold

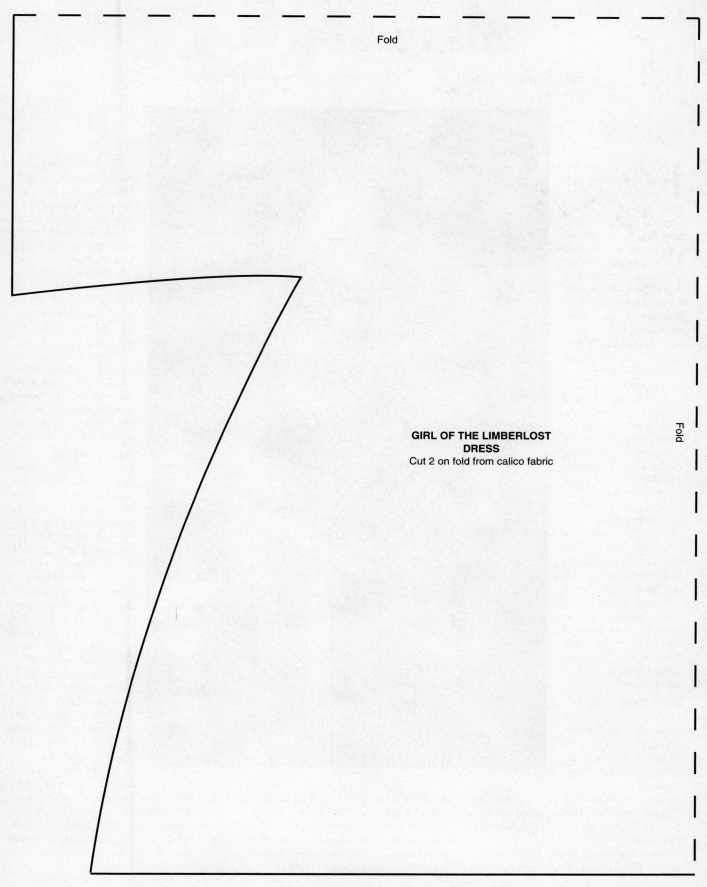

Fold

GIRL OF THE LIMBERLOST
DRESS
Cut 2 on fold from calico fabric

Fold

Sissy Starling

Make a cloth doll or venture into sculpture—the choice is yours!

It's true, of course—there's nothing new under the sun. And, even though I don't "get out much," I feel I have had a fairly broad exposure to the world of dollmaking through my affiliation over the past four years with House of White Birches doll publications. It may have been done before, but I have never seen a doll constructed like Sissy Starling. Her design is, at least to me, quite unique.

I have long enjoyed working with fabric, including dollmaking, and while I have been greatly intrigued by sculpting media, I never ventured into this realm. In retrospect, it seems that the many sculpting media on the market today make this art form so easy, accessible and affordable, anyone can attempt it. However, in my case and perhaps in yours, with busy schedules and many demands, it is so much easier to stay with the familiar. So when Sissy Starling happened along I thought, "Now is my chance!"

Basic Cloth Doll

Sissy Starling is the creation of Sonja Sandell, who designs for Hickety-Pickety. She recently submitted several photographs to *Doll World* for consideration. They were all nice cloth designs, but Sissy Starling stood out from the rest. She was obviously more than just a cloth doll!

Sissy Starling starts as a cloth doll with a muslin body. Her country charm is appealing of itself, but she takes on the additional charm of primitive folk art when papier-mâché is applied over the cloth body. The truly delightful part about this design is that the papier-mâché is entirely up to the discretion of the dollmaker—it's optional.

There is nothing complicated about this doll. Her head and body are one piece, formed from front and back pieces of muslin. The body pattern gives the contour of the hair, so that, if desired, this little dolly may simply be painted. If you choose to apply papier-mâché, the only sculpting really needed is for the nose.

Arms and legs are basic and are connected to the doll only at the dress sleeves and pantaloon legs, so even the assembly is simple. These may also be papier-mâchéd.

Papier-Mâché

Having never worked with papier-mâché before (or at least not since high school when we soaked strips of newspaper in paste for the homecoming floats!), I was amazed—and relieved—at how easy it is. The pattern calls for Celluclay prepackaged papier-mâché mix. It comes in a block, sort of, and all you need to do is mix it with water and knead.

I purchased a 1-pound package, and used such a little bit of it, I have plenty left for experimenting with future projects. I may have made it slightly thick, but it applied easily and was easy to work with. I think I may have been able to create a somewhat smoother surface if the papier-mâché had been a thinner consistency. But, as Sonja advises in her instructions, it's easier to add more water than to take it out. At any rate, it worked.

Preparation

Before covering with the papier-mâché, it is necessary to apply white glue to the muslin body parts. Then you smear on the papier-mâché and let it dry. It must be thoroughly dry before painting—I let mine dry overnight to be sure.

I discovered, when I began painting, that I had missed covering a few spots. Oh, well! Following Sonja's advice, I just painted over them and no one is the wiser. She emphatically states that she does things the easiest way possible, and the first thing to understand when using her patterns is that everything does *not* have to be perfect. It is those slight imperfections which make each doll unique.

Finishing

Her instructions are very friendly and laid-back. For example, while offering tips on what paint and stain to use, she encourages you to use whatever you have on hand. That I can do!

I found myself in short supply of black acrylic paint, so blended the colors I had to come up with Sissy's auburn brown hair and gray shoes. I decided green eyes would complement her hair nicely. After the body, arms and legs are painted, and the paint has thoroughly dried, Sonja applies dark oak or walnut oil-based wood stain for antiquing. Well, I discovered I didn't have any of that, either, but I did have some acrylic antiquing gel—so we happily made do.

Accessories

Now, Sonja gives instructions for making a 1¾" x 5¼" birdhouse from a ¾" piece of wood. It makes a very cute addition to the doll, but my woodcrafting skill leaves much to be desired, so I opted for a purchased house. It is not quite the same effect, but gives the general impression.

The little bird under her arm is supposed to be painted muslin; however, I had a small amount of papier-mâché left, so I papier-mâchéd it too! It's a good thing I hadn't mixed up more than I did; who knows what else I might have covered!

Thanks to Sissy Starling, I have taken that wobbly first step into the world of doll sculpting—with no casualties! It is a wonderful thing when your first attempt at something new is a successful one. I encourage all who want to broaden their dollmaking skills to make Sissy Starling for themselves. But don't let anyone else know how easy she was to make!

To order Sissy Starling contact Sonja J. Sandell, Hickety-Pickety, 906 S. Washington, Wellington, KS 67152, (316) 326–7281. Additional cloth, papier-mâché and wood patterns and unfinished wood accessories are available. Send $2 for color catalog. **DW**

Make Your Own Greeting Cards

Continued from page 46

On the opposite side from the window, set up your mirror, white tag board or aluminum foil-covered cardboard so that light from the window is bounced back onto the dolls.

Drape the area with your backdrop cloth or paper, making sure it is wrinkle-free. Check the area through the viewfinder of your camera and make sure the backdrop covers every area that your camera will actually see. Make sure your background is clean and smooth and contrasts with the scene you are setting up. Don't, for instance, photograph a doll dressed in white against a white background. She'll disappear!

I most often use deep sky blue for a background, but you may want to try other colors for different effects. Using a black background will make your doll appear to be floating in space.

Avoid colors with a lot of green in them, such as teal and evergreen. The only green I have found that prints well is a very bright spring green. White is also a difficult color to print, and will often show up on finished pictures as very light gray or blue.

Display Your Dolls

Now arrange your dolls on the backdrop. When you have a scene arranged that you think will make a good card, check it very carefully through the camera viewfinder. Don't let yourself see the tableau as it appears in your imagination. See it as it will actually appear to your camera.

Is the background area fully covered by your cloth or paper? Does the scene balance nicely within the frame of your camera's viewfinder? If you have several dolls in the scene, are they arranged so their shadows do not fall over each other?

What's important now is not how the display looks to you, but how it looks to the eye of your camera. Ask yourself if the picture will look better framed horizontally or vertically. Would the scene look better if it had fewer details in it? Sometimes simpler is better. When you've really examined your display and decided on a final arrangement, you're ready to take the picture.

Load Your Camera

Load your camera with ASA 100 film. You won't need a flash, as you are using the available light for illumination. You have examined the scene through the viewfinder and chosen how close you will hold the camera and how you will frame it.

Determine whether or not you will be able to hold the camera perfectly steady as you expose the film. If you need some help holding the camera still and do not have a tripod, you may want to set up a ladder facing the scene and rest your camera on one of the steps.

You could also set up an ironing board and use it as a stable platform for your camera. Take a look around the house and you will certainly find something that will act as a platform during the few seconds your camera's eye is open.

Take the Picture

Now, shoot your picture. When I take my photographs, I "bracket the shots"—I choose what I think will be my best shot and then set the f-stop a little above and a little below that setting.

For instance, I usually get my best shots at f-stop 11, so I bracket that shot between f-8 and f-16. It gives me a better chance of getting a perfect exposure. Also, try taking your photo from different angles, with the camera aimed not only straight on to the scene, but also a little above the scene looking down, and a little below the scene looking up. I use a roll of film with 12 shots on it, and I use the entire film shooting just one picture for a greeting card. By moving around and trying different angles, and different exposures, I am usually able to get at least one good photograph.

Assemble Your Cards

After you have your film developed and have chosen your best photograph, there are several different ways you can make it into a greeting card. At Christmas, almost all film developers offer a service that will print your photo on a glossy stock card, usually with your choice of imprinted greetings. In 1995, I paid less than $20 to have 60 cards printed at a major discount department store. These came with envelopes and a special pen to write on photos. I would have spent more buying mass-produced greetings at a card shop!

You can also buy self-adhesive postcard backings at many camera and almost all fine-art supply stores. These are plain white cards, marked with an area to place the stamp and address, just as you see on the backs of commercial postcards. You simply peel off the paper on the sticky side of the card and press it to the back of your photograph, and *voila!* you have an instant custom postcard.

At these same stores, you can also find paper greeting cards with a front area open for the insertion of your own photograph. These may be done with special greetings inside, or left blank for your own best wishes.

You can also use mat or tag board from an art supply store to cut simple frames for your own cards. Use an artist's razor knife and a hard-edged ruler to make clean cuts on the mat board, and affix your photo with a glue stick. It's a simple, inexpensive and attractive presentation.

Don't hesitate to ask the people in any fine-art supply store for help. They'll be happy to show you all the different supplies they have for making your own cards. It's so much fun, you may never buy a greeting card again! **DW**

Doll Shows

UNITED STATES

■ ARIZONA

PAYSON—JULY 20: Payson Annual Doll Show & Sale. Payson Middle School, 304 S. Meadow. SASE to Phyllis Best, 804 E. Phoenix St., Payson, AZ 85541; (520) 474–3107.

■ ARKANSAS

EUREKA SPRINGS—SEPT. 14: Eureka Springs Doll & Toy Show & Sale by M & M Productions. 10 am–4 pm. Convention Center behind Inn of the Ozarks, Best Western Motel, Rte. 62 W. Adm $3; youths, $1. SASE to Mrs. George Bromstad, #5 Table Rock Dr., Eureka Springs, AR 72632; (501) 253–2244; (501) 253–8306.

■ CALIFORNIA

ANAHEIM—JULY 7: Fourth of July Celebration with Barbie® & Friends by Dolls, Etc. 10 am–3 pm. Disneyland Pacific Hotel, 1717 S. West St. Adm $4. SASE to Dolls, Etc., Katherine Burrows, P.O. Box 419, Torrance, CA 90508; (310) 328–8420.

CORONA—JULY 12–14: Main Event Collectibles Show by Main Event. McKinley Home Center, 2180 Nevada, #190. Fri., 5–10 pm; Sat. & Sun., 10 am–5 pm. Adm free. SASE to Main Event, 2180 Nevada St., Ste. 190, Corona, CA 91719; (909) 371–4451.

SAN DIEGO—JULY 13: Down on Grandpa's Farm by North Park Doll Collectors. 10 am–3 pm. North Park Recreation Center Gym, 4044 Idaho. Adm free. Jo Barckley, (619) 286–0355.

VENTURA—JULY 13 & 14: Ventura Dolls, Bears, Supplies & Collectibles Show & Sale by The Miller Production Group. Sat., 10 am–5 pm; Sun., 11 am–4 pm. Ventura Fairgrounds, 10 W. Harbor Blvd. #101—California St. or Ventura Ave. exit. Fairgrounds parking fee $1. Adm $5; with coupon, $4; 6–12, $2. SASE to The Miller Production Group, P.O. Box 967, Rancho Santa Fe, CA 92067; (619) 756–3275.

SACRAMENTO—JULY 20: Judi Lee's Doll Show by Judi Lee. 10 am–4 pm. Scottish Rite Temple, 6151 H St. Adm $3.50. SASE to Judi Lee's, P.O. Box 5366, Sonora, CA 95370; (209) 532–1707.

ANAHEIM—JULY 21: Peterson's Show & Sale featuring Barbie® Dolls by Barbara Peterson. 10 am–3 pm. Disneyland Hotel, 1150 W. Cerritos Ave. Adm $5; 5 & under, $2. (714) 525–8420.

VALLEJO—JULY 27: Nancy Jo's Doll Sale by Nancy Jo Schreeder. 9 am–4 pm. Vallejo Fairgrounds, Fairgrounds Dr. across from Marine World. Adm $5.25; early adm, $15. SASE to Vallejo Doll Sale, Nancy Jo Schreeder, 305 Robinson St., Martinez, CA 94553; (510) 229–4190.

CORONA—AUG. 9–11: Main Event Collectibles Show by Main Event. McKinley Home Center, 2180 Nevada, #190. Fri., 5–10 pm; Sat. & Sun., 10 am–5 pm. Adm free. SASE to Main Event, 2180 Nevada St., Ste. 190, Corona, CA 91719; (909) 371–4451.

SAN DIEGO—AUG. 10 & 11: Linda's Teddy Bear, Doll & Antique Toy Show & Sale. Sat., 10:30 am–4 pm; Sun., 10 am–3 pm. Scottish Rite Center, 1895 Camino Del Rio S. Adm $5; early adm, Sat., 8:30 am–10:30 am, $15. SASE to Linda Mullins, P.O. Box 2327, Carlsbad, CA 92018; (619) 434–7444; Fax, (619) 434–0154.

SAN RAFAEL—AUG. 17: Marin County Summer Doll Show by Golden Gate Shows. 10 am–4 pm. Marin County Civic Center Exhibition Hall, Hwy. 101 to N. San Pedro Rd., East. Adm $4; under 12, $2; under 5, free. SASE to Fern Loiacono, Ross, CA 94957–1208; (415) 459–1998; Fax, (415) 459–0827.

COSTA MESA—AUG. 17 & 18: Costa Mesa Dolls, Bears Supplies & Collectibles Show & Sale by Miller Production Group. Sat., 10 am–5 pm; Sun., 11 am–4 pm. Orange County Fair and Exposition Center, 88 Fair Dr. Adm $5; with coupon, $4; 6–12, $2. SASE to Miller Production Group, P.O. Box 967, Rancho Santa Fe, CA 92067; (619) 756–3275.

ANAHEIM—AUG. 18: Peterson's Show & Sale featuring Barbie® Dolls by Barbara Peterson. 10 am–3 pm. Disneyland Hotel, 1150 W. Cerritos Ave. Adm $5; 5 & under, $2. (714) 525–8420.

OAKHURST—AUG. 31: Doll Sale of Dolls, Bears & Miniatures by Yosemite Mountain Dollers Doll Club. 10 am–4 pm. Community Center Building, Road 425B. Adm $3; children, $2. Jim Kirin, (209) 683–5075.

SANTA ROSA—SEPT. 7: Santa Rosa Fall Doll Show by Golden Gate Shows. 10 am–4 pm. Sonoma County Fairgrounds, Hwy. 101 to Hwy. 12, east to first off ramp (S. E St.) Adm $4; under 12, $2; under 5, free. SASE to Fern Loiacono, Ross, CA 94957–1208; (415) 459–1998; Fax, (415) 459–0827.

SACRAMENTO—SEPT. 8: Forever Young All Barbie® Doll Show by Don Smith & Bahama Leaf Productions. 9 am–4 pm. Radisson Hotel, 500 Leisure Ln. Adm $5. Rochester. SASE to Don Smith, P.O. Box 626, Shelton, WA 98584.

CORONA—SEPT. 13–15: Main Event Collectibles Show by Main Event. McKinley Home Center, 2180 Nevada, #190. Fri., 5–10 pm; Sat. & Sun., 10 am–5 pm. Adm free. SASE to Main Event, 2180 Nevada St., Ste. 190, Corona, CA 91719; (909) 371–4451.

ANAHEIM—SEPT. 14: Peterson's Show & Sale featuring Barbie® Dolls by Barbara Peterson. 10 am–3 pm. Disneyland Hotel, 1150 W. Cerritos Ave. Adm $5; 5 & under, $2. (714) 525–8420.

SAN JOSE—SEPT. 14: San Jose Fall Doll Show by Golden Gate Shows. 10 am–4 pm. Santa Clara Fairgrounds, Hwy. 101 to Tully Rd. West. Adm $4; under 12, $2; under 5, free. SASE to Fern Loiacono, Ross, CA 94957–1208; (415) 459–1998; Fax, (415) 459–0827.

■ COLORADO

CORTEZ—JULY 20: Four Corners Doll, Teddy, Toy & Miniature Show by Four Corners Doll Club. 9 am–4 pm. Cortex Conference Center, 2121 E. Main St. Adm free. SASE to Norma Howell, 819 Brookside Dr., Cortez, CO 81321; (970) 565–9517.

■ FLORIDA

SARASOTA—JULY 13 & 14: 17th Annual Doll & Bear Show & Sale by Steve Schroeder. Sat., 10 am–5 pm; Sun., 11 am–4 pm. Sarasota Municipal Auditorium, 801 N. Tamiami Trail (U.S. Hwy. 41). Adm $3.50; two-day pass, $5; under 12, free with adult. SASE to Steve Schroeder, 3100 Harvest Ln., Kissimmee, FL 34744; (407) 957–6392; Fax, (407) 957–9427.

MELBOURNE—AUG. 17: Sixth Annual Doll & Bear Show & Sale by Steve Schroeder. Sat., 10 am–5 pm. Azan Shrine Temple, 1591 W. Eau Gallie Blvd., I-95, Exit 72, 3½ miles east. Adm $3; under 12, free with adult. SASE to Steve Schroeder, 3100 Harvest Ln., Kissimmee, FL 34744; (407) 957–6392; Fax, (407) 957–9427.

JACKSONVILLE—AUG. 24: River City Doll & Bear Show. 10 am–4 pm. Morocco Temple, St. John's Bluff Rd. Adm $3.50; under 12, $1. SASE to M. Hill, 13030 Bent Pine Ct. E, Jacksonville, FL 32246; (904) 221–1235.

■ GEORGIA

ATLANTA—SEPT. 8: Barbie® Goes to … Atlanta by Joe & Marl Shows. 10 am–4 pm. The Renaissance at the Atlanta Airport, 4736 Best Rd. Adm $5; under 12, $2. Marl, (941) 751–6275; Joe, (213) 953–6490.

■ HAWAII

AINALOA, PUNA DISTRICT—JULY 6: Doll & Teddy Bear Sale by East Hawaii Doll Collectors Club. 7:30 am–12 pm.

■ PANAMA CITY BEACH—SEPT. 7:

Treasures Old & New Doll Show by Panama City Doll Club. 9:30 am–4 pm. Bay Point Yacht Club, 4700 Bay Point Rd. Adm $2; under 12, free. SASE to Jo Patterson, 1428 Beck Ave., Panama City, FL 32401; (904) 872–0008.

TALLAHASSEE—SEPT. 14: Babes in Babyland Doll & Bear Show & Sale by Tallahassee Doll Collectors. 10 am–4 pm. Elks Lodge, 276 N. Magnolia Ave. Adm $3. SASE to Cathy Carver, 8620 Heartwood, Tallahassee, FL 32312; (904) 668–3880.

KISSIMMEE—SEPT. 14 & 15: Second Annual Doll & Bear Show & Sale by Steve Schroeder. Sat., 10 am–5 pm; Sun., 11 am–4 pm. Agricultural Building, 1901 E. Irlo Bronson Memorial Hwy., U.S. Hwy. 192 (The Road to the Worlds). Adm $3; two-day pass, $5; under 12, free with adult. SASE to Steve Schroeder, 3100 Harvest Ln., Kissimmee, FL 34744; (407) 957–6392; Fax, (407) 957–9427.

Ainaloa Community Longhouse, Puna District, Big Island of Hawaii. Ruth Sleightholm, (808) 982–9355.

■ ILLINOIS

GENESEO—JULY 13: Geneseo's Annual Doll Show & Sale by Doris Kneen & Cheryl Benoodt. 10 am–4 pm. Deck Plaza Hotel, I-80, Exit 19. Adm $2; children, 75 cents. SASE to Doris Kneen, 212 College Ave., Geneseo, IL 61254; (309) 944–4076.

NAPERVILLE—JULY 28: Antique & Collectible Doll & Bear Show & Sale by Gould & Gallup Productions. 9 am–4 pm. Holiday Inn, 1801 N. Naperville Rd. Adm $4; under 12, free. SASE to Gallup & Gould, 28 W 491 87th St., Naperville, IL 60564; (798) 355–0574.

COUNTRYSIDE—AUG. 4: 17th Annual Storyland Doll & Bear Show & Sale by Storyland Doll Club. 10 am–4 pm. Operating Engineers Hall, 6200 Joliet Rd., Rtes. 66 & 45 (Mannheim & LaGrange Rds.). Adm $3. SASE to J. Vidinich, 12240 Rexford, Alsip, IL 60658; (708) 368–7628.

ROCKFORD—AUG. 10: Rockford Summer Doll, Toy & Bear Show & Sale by JoAnn Reynolds. 9 am–4 pm. Forest Hills Lodge, 9900 Forest Hills Rd. Adm $2.50. SASE to JoAnn Reynolds, 6058 Daysville Rd., Oregon, IL 61061.

LINCOLN—AUG. 24: Fourth Annual Doll & Bear Show & Sale by Logan County Dollers. 9:30 am–4 pm. Moose Lodge, 521 N. Kickapoo St. Adm $2;

Doll Shows

under 12, free with adult. SASE to Barbara Morrow, Rte. 1, Box 308, Clinton, IL 61727.

ST. CHARLES—AUG. 25: Doll & Bear Show by A. Willmann-Gould & Gallup. 8:30 am–4 pm. Kane County Fairgrounds, Randall Rd. Adm $4; under 12, free. SASE to Willmann's, P.O. Box 814, Sugar Grove, IL 60554; Gould & Gallup, (708) 264–0004; Fax, (708) 264–2737.

HILLSIDE—SEPT. 8: First Annual Teddy Bears on Parade in Super Sunday at Hillside Show & Sale by Bright Star Promotions. 10 am–4:30 pm. Hillside Holiday Inn, I-294 to I-290E. to M 4400 Frontage Rd. Adm $4; 12 & under, $1.50. SASE to Valerie Rogers, Bright Star Promotions, 3428 Hillvale Rd., Louisville, KY 40241-2756; (502) 423–STAR.

■ INDIANA

LAGRANGE—JULY 13: Doll Show & Sale by Sharing Doll Club. 10 am–4 pm. 1055 E 075 N. Adm $2. SASE to Iva Merrifield, 210½ W. Michigan, LaGrange, IN 46761.

INDIANAPOLIS—AUG. 24: 20th Century Doll Club Show. 8:30 am–4:30 pm. U.A.W. #111 Union Hall, 431 S. Shortridge Rd. Adm $2; children, $1. SASE to Peggy Herdrich, 8612 Jamaica Ct., Indianapolis, IN 46219; (317) 898–3654.

FORT WAYNE—SEPT. 14: Fourth Annual Teddy Bears on Parade in Fort Wayne Show & Sale by Bright Star Promotions. 10 am–4:30 pm. Fort Wayne Marriott, I-69 at Coldwater Rd., 305 E. Washington Center Rd. Adm $4; 12 & under, $1.50. SASE to Valerie Rogers, Bright Star Promotions, 3428 Hillvale Rd., Louisville, KY 40241-2756; (502) 423–STAR.

LOGANSPORT—SEPT. 14: Doll Show & Sale by Dolls Unlimited. 10 am–4 pm. Holiday Inn, U.S. 24 East. Adm $2; children, $1. SASE to Carol Jensen, 1315 E. Fourth St., Rochester, IN 46975.

FORT WAYNE—SEPT. 15: 15th Annual Summit City Miniatures Show & Sale by Bright Star Promotions. 10 am–4:30 pm. Fort Wayne Marriott, I-69, Exit 112A, Coldwater Rd. Adm $4; 12 & under, $1.50. SASE to Bright Star Promotions, 3428 Hillvale Rd., Louisville, KY 40241-2756; (502) 423–STAR.

■ IOWA

CEDAR RAPIDS—AUG. 25: School Days 1996 by Old Capitol Doll Club of Iowa. 9 am–4 pm. Teamster's Building, 5000 J St. S.W. Adm $2.50; children, $1. SASE to Larry Bailey, 1716 Baker Ave., West Branch, IA 52358; (319) 643–2441.

MAQUOKETA—SEPT. 8: Annual Fall Doll, Toy & Bear Show by Dora Pitts. 9 am–4 pm. Jackson County Fairgrounds, Hwys. 62 & 64. Adm $2.50; under 12, free. SASE to Dora Pitts, 4697 155th St., Clinton, IA 52732; (319) 242–0139.

OTTUMWA—SEPT. 14: 10th Annual YWCA Doll & Toy Show

& Sale by YWCA Doll Club (UFDC). 9 am–4 pm. Ottumwa Coliseum, 102 Church St. Adm $2; children, 50 cents. SASE to Wanda Selby, 726 Johnson, Ottumwa, IA 52501; (515) 684–7213.

■ KANSAS

WINFIELD—AUG. 10: Sixth Annual Walnut Valley Doll Show & Sale, Juried Show & Gallery Exhibit by Winfield Arts & Humanities Council. 10 am–4 pm. Winfield Community Center at Baden Square, 700 Gary. Adm $2. SASE to Ann Moore Laws, Winfield Arts & Humanities Council, 700 Gary, Suite A, Winfield, KS 67156-3135.

WICHITA—AUG. 24: Third Annual Doll Show & Sale by Cessna Employees Doll Club. 9 am–5 pm. Cessna Activity Center, 2744 George Washington Blvd. Adm $2; 10 & under, free. Linda, (316) 776–0291.

KANSAS CITY—SEPT. 1: 17th Annual Fall Kansas City Toy & Doll Show. 10 am–4 pm. Jack Reardon Civic Center, Fifth & Minnesota. Adm $2; children, free with adult. SASE to Bob & Judy Condray, 1005 W. 11th, Concordia, KS 66901; (913) 243–3774 or (913) 455–3440.

■ LOUISIANA

LAFAYETTE—AUG. 24 & 25: Les Jolie Poupee Des Acadians by Les Jolie Poupee Des Acadian Doll Club. 10 am–5 pm. Hotel Acadiana, 1901 Pinhook Rd. Adm $3. SASE to Linda Ewalt, P.O. Box 96, Lacassine, LA 70650.

HOUMA—SEPT. 28 & 29: Doll Lovers Club Fourth Annual Show. Quality Inn, 1400 W. Tunnel Blvd. SASE to Ramona Charpentier, 801 Natalie Dr., Houma, LA 70364; (504) 876–6797.

■ MAINE

BELFAST—AUG. 18: Dolls, Bears & Miniatures Show by Coastal Maine Doll Club & DAR. 10 am–4 pm. Belfast Armory, Rte. 1. Adm $2. SASE to Jill Goodwin, 84 Union St., Belfast, ME 04915.

■ MARYLAND

GREENBELT—JULY 14: Third Annual Teddy Bears on Parade in Greenbelt Show & Sale by Bright Star Promotions. 10 am–4 pm. Greenbelt Marriott Inn, I-495 to Kenilworth N., 6400 Ivy Ln. Adm $4; 12 & under, $1.50. SASE to Valerie Rogers, Bright Star Promotions, 3428 Hillvale Rd., Louisville, KY 40241-2756; (502) 423–STAR.

SAVAGE—AUG. 3: 10th Annual Summer Bear & Doll Show & Sale by Savage Mill Foundation. 10 am–5:30 pm. Historic Savage Mill. Adm free. SASE to Savage Mill Foundation, Historic Savage Mill, Mill Box 2022, Savage, MD 20763; (800) 788–MILL.

WALDORF—SEPT. 14: Southern Maryland Doll Club Annual Doll Show & Sale. 10 am–4 pm. John Hanson Middle School, Crain Highway. Adm $3.50.

SASE to Toni Corley, 4752 Hummingbird Dr., Waldorf, MD 20603; (301) 645–3733.

■ MICHIGAN

KALAMAZOO—JULY 14: Fall Doll Show & Sale by Jean Canaday. 9:30 am–4 pm. Kalamazoo Fairgrounds, Lake St., I-94, Sprinkle Rd. Exit. Adm $3; under 12, free. SASE to Jean Canaday, P.O. Box 127, Holt, MI 48842; (517) 694–3663.

GRAND RAPIDS—JULY 20: 12th Annual Grand Rapids Miniatures Show & Sale by Bright Star Promotions. 10 am–4:30 pm. Hilton Inn Airport, 4747 28th St. Adm $4; 12 & under, $1.50. SASE to Bright Star Promotions, 3428 Hillvale Rd., Louisville, KY 40241-2756; (502) 423–STAR.

ANN ARBOR—JULY 21: Eighth Annual Teddy Bears on Parade in Ann Arbor Show & Sale by Bright Star Promotions. 10 am–4:30 pm. Weber's Inn, I-94, Exit 172. Adm $4; 12 & under, $1.50. SASE to Bright Star Promotions, 3428 Hillvale Rd., Louisville, KY 40241-2756; (502) 423–STAR.

DETROIT—AUG. 9 & 10: Indigo of the Harlem Renaissance Doll Show & Sale by Brown Rice and Howell Enterprises. Fri., 10 am–11 pm; Sat., 12–9 pm. YWCA Executive Building, 1411 E. Jefferson. Adm $5; children, free. SASE to Marsha Taylor, 486 Marlborough, Detroit, MI 48215; (313) 824–3302.

BRIDGMAN—SEPT. 7 & 8: Dolls, Dolls, Dolls Show by Cook Energy Information Center. 10 am–5 pm. Cook Energy Information Center, I-94, Exit 16, Bridgman, 3½ miles north on Red Arrow Hwy. Adm free. Dolly Krieger, (800) 548–2555.

SAGINAW—SEPT. 8: Saginaw Doll Show by Debbie Wilinski. 10 am–4 pm. Knights of Columbus Hall, 4840 Shattuck Rd. Adm $3; 12 & under, $1. SASE to Debbie Wilinski, P.O. Box 185, Kawkawlin, MI 48631; (517) 684–6891.

■ MINNESOTA

MORA—AUG. 3: Mora Doll Show & Sale by Anderson & Dorsey. 10 am–4 pm. Zion Lutheran Church, 401 S. Hwy. 65. Adm $2; under 12, 50 cents. SASE to Bette Anderson, 222 Second St., Mora, MN 55051.

BEMIDJI—AUG. 11: Eighth Annual Dolls, Toys, Teddy Bears & Miniature Show & Sale by Northwoods Doll Club. 10 am–4 pm. Northern Inn Convention Center, Hwy. 2 West. Adm $3; seniors, $2; under 12, free with adult. SASE to Sharon Geisen, 5827 Balsam Rd. N.W., Bemidji, MN 56601-7726; (218) 751–8277.

WADENA—AUG. 24: Miss USA Doll Pageant Show & Sale. 9 am–2 pm. National Guard Armory, Hwy. 71. Adm $1. Vonnie Perius, (218) 631–2270; (218) 631–4392.

■ MISSOURI

LAKE OZARK—AUG. 17: Eighth Annual 1996 Dolls &

Crafts Sale by Hello Dollee's Doll Club. 9 am–4 pm. Lake Ozarks Lions Club, Bus. Hwy. 54, ¾ mile from Bus. Hwy. 54 & Hwy. 54 junction. Adm free. SASE to Eileen Wallace, 5 S. Grand, Eldon, MO 65026; (573) 392–1601.

EL DORADO SPRINGS— SEPT. 14: Fourth Annual Show & Sale by Wonder City Doll Club. 10 am–4 pm. El Dorado Springs Commnunity Building. Adm free. SASE to Kay Smith, Rte. 1, Box 30G, Osceola, MO 64776; (417) 646–8616.

■ NEVADA

RENO—AUG. 31 & SEPT. 1: Judi Lee's Doll Show by Judi Lee. Sat., 10 am–5 pm; Sun., 10 am–4 pm. Reno Convention Center, North Hall, Section B. Adm $4; seniors & children, $3. SASE to Judi Lee's, P.O. Box 5366, Sonora, CA 95370; (209) 532–1707.

■ NEW HAMPSHIRE

GILFORD—AUG. 18: 14th Annual Lakes Region Doll Show & Sale. 9:30 am–3 pm. Gilford Middle High School, Belknap Mountain Rd. from Rte. 11A. Adm $2; under 12, $1. Alice Ortkales, (603) 524–0129 or (603) 524–2925.

■ NEW JERSEY

TRENTON—JULY 13: 18th Annual Christmas in July Doll & Toy Show & Sale by Delaware Valley Doll Club of New Jersey. 10 am–5 pm. Colonial Fire Hall, 801 Kuser Rd. Adm $3.

MULLICA HILL—AUG. 17: Follow the Yellow Brick Road Doll Show & Sale by Yellow Brick Road Dolls & Toy Museum. 10 am–4 pm. 34 S. Main St., Rte. 45. Adm $3. SASE to Dorothy Tancraitor, P.O. Box 306, Mullica Hill, NJ 08062.

■ NEW YORK

JAMESTOWN—JULY 13: Childhood Dreams XIII Doll Show, Sale & Competition by Doll Study Club of Jamestown. 10 am–4 pm. Holiday Inn, W. Fourth St. Adm $2; under 12, free with adult. SASE to Nancy Harner, 225 Indiana Ave., Jamestown, NY 14701; (716) 484–7263.

ALEXANDER—SEPT. 8: Fairlands Doll Show by Fairland Dollis. 10 am–4 pm. Alexander Firemen's Recreation Hall. Adm $3. SASE to Sue Spink, 1125 Rte. 98, Attica, NY 14011.

MELVILLE—SEPT. 8: 11th Annual Spring Festival Show & Sale by CSR Promotions. 9:30 am–4 pm. Huntington Hilton Grand Ballroom, Rte. 110 (Broad Hollow Rd.), L.I.E. (I-495), Exit 49 South. Adm $3; under 12, $1. SASE to CSR Promotions, P.O. Box 1211, Skyland, NC 28776; (704) 272–7732.

ROCHESTER—SEPT. 15: Doll Lovers Doll & Teddy Bear Show by H & D Toys. 10 am–4 pm. Gateway Center, 4853 W. Henrietta Rd., 3236 E. Henrietta Rd., Henrietta, GA 14467. Adm $3.

■ NORTH CAROLINA

ASHEVILLE—AUG. 10: Eighth Annual Show by Doll Dreamers of WNC. 10 am–4 pm. National Guard Armory, 1 Brevard Rd. Adm $2.50; under 12, free with paying adult. SASE to Alline Rhodes, 390 Hoopers Creek Rd., Fletcher, NC 28732; (704) 684–8170.

CLEMMONS—AUG. 24: Doll Show & Sale by Carolina Hobby Expo. 10 am–4 pm. Ramada Inn, I-40, Exit 184. Adm $3; under 12, free. SASE to Carolina Hobby Expo, 3452 Odell School Rd., Concord, NC 28027.

ASHEVILLE—SEPT. 14: 15th Annual Doll Show & Sale by Blue Ridge Doll Club. 9:30 am–3:30 pm. National Guard Armory, I-40, Exit 47, Brevard Rd. Adm $2; under 12, free. SASE to Ann McChesney, 80 Wagon Trail Rd., Black Mountain, NC 28711; (704) 669–7381.

■ NORTH DAKOTA

BISMARCK—JULY 7: Gateway Mall Doll Show & Sale by North Dakota Doll Club. 12–5 pm. Gateway Mall, I-94 & Hwy. 83 N. Adm free. SASE to Angie Dietrich, 11001 145th St. S.E., Bismarck, ND 58504-4101; (701) 673–3222.

GRAND FORKS—SEPT. 1: Annual Holiday Doll Show & Sale. 11 am–5 pm. Grand Forks Holiday Inn ballroom. Adm $2.50; children, $1. SASE to Janice Birkholz, 1605 Sixth St. N.W., Minot, ND 58703; (701) 839–6125.

■ OHIO

ARCHBOLD—AUG. 3 & 4: 16th Annual Doll Show & Sale by Sauder Village. Sat., 10 am–5 pm; Sun., 1–5 pm. Sauder Farm & Craft Village, Rte. 2. Adm (show & village) $9; seniors, $8.50; 6–16, $4.50. SASE to Sauder Farm & Craft Village, P.O. Box 235, Archbold, OH 43502; (800) 590–9755; e-mail, 10267.3365@compuserve.com.

COLUMBUS—AUG. 4: Annual Doll Show & Sale. 10 am–5 pm. Aladdin Temple, 3850 Stelzer Rd. Adm $3; under 12, $1.50. Vivian Ashbaugh, Box 579, Pataskala, OH 43062; (614) 587–4722.

FINDLAY—AUG. 18: Doll & Bear Show & Competition by Fort Findlay Doll Fanciers. 10 am–4 pm. 10040 U.S. Rte. 24 West. Adm $3; children, $1. SASE to Wanda Cusac, 5938 Cass Twp. Rd. 243, Findlay, OH 45840; (419) 424–5893.

ARCHBOLD—SEPT. 8: Top of Ohio Doll Show by Top of Ohio Doll Club. 10 am–5 pm. Four County Joint Vocational School, Rte. 66 & Rte. 34, 4 miles south of Archbold. Adm $2. SASE to Nancy Rosendaul, 18794 State Rd. 34, Bryan, OH 43506; (419) 636–7404; or June Grandey, 08016 State Rd. 249, Hicksville, OH 43526; (419) 658–2531.

LANCASTER—SEPT. 8: Fairfield County Doll Show & Sale by Three Sisters Productions.

Doll Shows

10 am–4 pm. Best Western Hotel, Rte. 33. Adm $2; under 12, $1. SASE to Gina Sheppard, 5990 Almina Dr., Galloway, OH 43119.

■ OREGON
REDMOND—SEPT. 13 & 14: Second Childhood Doll Show & Sale. Fri., 11 am–5 pm; Sat., 10 am–4 pm. Redmond VFW Hall. Adm $1. SASE to Wanda Ferguson, 6566 S. Stillman, Powell Butte, OR 47753.

■ PENNSYLVANIA
TANNERSVILLE—JULY 28: Fourth Annual Pocono Doll & Bear Show by B.T. Promotions. 10 am–4 pm. The Chateau at Camelback. Adm $4; children, $1.50. SASE to Rick Damour, R.R. 5, Box 5430, Saylorsburg, PA 18353; (717) 992–0254.

MONROEVILLE—SEPT. 13–15: 38th Annual Ceramic & Doll Expo by Pittsylvania Ceramic Guild. Fri. & Sat., 11 am–5 pm; Sun., 11 am–4 pm. Pittsburgh Expo Mart, Bus. Rte. 22. Adm $4. SASE to Shirle A. Balog, 14260 Caroline Dr., North Huntington, PA 15642-1208.

PITTSBURGH—SEPT. 15: Pittsburgh Ornament & Collectibles Show. 9 am–3:30 pm. Greentree Marriott, I-279, Exit 4. Adm $3. SASE to Rich Schachte, 1800 Freeport Rd., Arnold, PA 15068.

■ SOUTH CAROLINA
SANTEE—SEPT. 7: Doll & Bear Show by Brenda Welker. 10 am–4 pm. Ramada Inn. Adm $3. SASE to Brenda Welker, P.O. Box 1557, Tybee Island, GA 31328; (912) 786–5457.

■ TENNESSEE
LEBANON—JULY 13: 10th Annual Show by Jolly Dolls of Tennessee. 9 am–4 pm. James E. Ward Agriculture & Community Center, Wilson County Fairgrounds, 945 Baddour Pky. Adm $2; children, 50¢. Edna F. Anderson, (615) 683–8390.

MEMPHIS—AUG. 31: A Potpourri of Dolls by Southern Belles Doll Club. 9 am–4 pm. Youth Building, Mid-South Fairgrounds. Adm $3; children, $1. SASE to Donna Brown, 7165 Crestridge, Memphis, TN 38119; (901) 755–0701.

■ TEXAS
CORPUS CHRISTI—JULY 13: 15th Annual South Texas Doll, Toy & Bear Show & Sale by Jean Huff. 9 am–4 pm. Bay Front Plaza Convention Center, Shoreline Dr. Adm $3; children, $1. SASE to Jean Huff, Rte. 1, Box 173P, Mathis, TX 78368; (512) 547–3757.

AUSTIN—JULY 27: First Annual Teddy Bears on Parade in Austin Show & Sale by Bright Star Promotions. 10 am–4 pm. Doubletree Hotel. Adm $3; 12 & under, $1.50. SASE to Valerie Rogers, Bright Star Promotions, 3428 Hillvale Rd., Louisville, KY 40241-2756; (502) 423–STAR.

HOUSTON—JULY 28: Fourth Annual Greater Houston Miniatures Show & Sale by Bright Star Promotions. 10 am–4:30 pm. Marriott Inn at Greenspoint, I-45 at N. Sam Houston Pky. E. Adm $4; 12 & under, $1.50. SASE to Valerie Rogers, Bright Star Promotions, 3428 Hillvale Rd., Louisville, KY 40241-2756; (502) 423–STAR.

PLANO—AUG. 23 & 24: Annual Dallas Doll Expo by Dolls, Ceramics 'N' Such. Fri., 10 am–6 pm; Sat., 10 am–5 pm. Plano Center, 2000 E. Spring Creek Pky. Adm $4; seniors, $3; under 12, free with adult. SASE to Shirley Jenson, 11531 Burning Oaks Rd., Oklahoma City, OK 73150; (405) 739–0992; Fax, (405) 739–0993.

IRVING—AUG. 24: Barbie® Goes to ... Dallas by Joe & Marl Shows. 10 am–4 pm. Holiday Inn of Dallas/Fort Worth Airport South, 4440 W. Airport Freeway. Adm $5; under 12, $2. Marl, (941) 751–6275; Joe, (213) 953–6490.

■ VERMONT
BURLINGTON—JULY 21: Fourth Annual Summer Festival Doll & Teddy Bear Show & Sale by CSR Promotions. 9:30 am–4 pm. Sheraton Burlington Hotel & Conference Center, 870 Williston Rd., I-89, Exit 14W. Adm $3.50; under 12, $1. SASE to CSR Promotions, P.O. Box 1211, Skyland, NC 28776; (704) 274–7732.

■ VIRGINIA
MCLEAN—JULY 21: Barbie® Goes to ... Washington, D.C. by Joe & Marl Shows. 10 am–4 pm. Westpark Hotel, 8401 Westpark Dr. Adm $5; under 12, $2. Marl, (941) 751–6275; Joe, (213) 953–6490.

LYNCHBURG—SEPT. 7: Third Annual Doll Show by Old & New Doll Club of Central Virginia. 10 am–4 pm. Salvation Army Gymnasium, 2215 Park Ave. Adm $2; children with adult, free; children must be accompanied by parent. SASE to Anne Keeney, 179 F Mistover Dr., Rte. 1, Monroe, VA 24574; (804) 384–3731.

■ WASHINGTON
TACOMA—JULY 27: Doll & Toy Extravaganza by Michele Karl. 10 am–4 pm; early adm, 9–10 am. Tacoma Dome. Adm (both shows) $4; early adm, $8; under 12, free. SASE to Michele Karl, Lynchwood, WA 98036; (206) 744–0983.

OCEAN SHORES—SEPT. 14: Doll, Bear & Toy Show by Two Sails Productions. 10 am–5 pm. Ocean Shores Convention Center. Adm $2.50, seniors & under $2. SASE to Suzanne Morris, 15 Westview Dr., Hoquiam, WA 98550.

QUINCY—SEPT. 14: Cradle Doll Club Show by Farmer Consumer Awareness Day. 9:30 am–4 pm. Quincy High School Gym. Adm free. SASE to Velma F. Sivey, 109 D St. S.E., Apt. 102, Quincy, WA 98848.

■ WISCONSIN
ALGOMA—JULY 12 & 13: 32nd Annual Doll & Teddy Bear Show & Sale by Algoma United Methodist Church. Algoma Youth Center, 620 Lake St. Adm $2.50; 6–12, $1; under 6, free. SASE to Al Hansen, N 96 W 20235 County Line Rd., Menomonee Falls, WI 53051-7133; (414) 255–4465; Fax, (414) 255–5884.

MADISON—JULY 28: Orphans in the Attic Doll, Toy & Bear Show & Sale by Marge Hansen. 9:30 am–4 pm. Ramada Inn, 3521 Evan Acres Rd., I-90, Exit 142B. Adm $3; 6–12, $1. SASE to Marge Hansen, N 96 W 20235 County Line Rd., Menomonee Falls, WI 53051-7133; (414) 255–4465.

WOODRUFF—AUG. 3: 18th Annual Show & Sale by Enchanted Doll Club of Eagle River. 10 am–4 pm. 412 Balsam St. Adm $2. SASE to Barb Spiess, 4971 Rummels Rd., Conover, WI 54519.

MILWAUKEE—SEPT. 8: Orphans in the Attic Doll & Bear Show & Sale by Marge Hansen. 9:30 am–4 pm. Serb Hall, 5101 W. Oklahoma Ave. Adm $3; 6–12, $1. SASE to Marge Hansen, N 96 W 20235 County Line Rd., Menomonee Falls, WI 53051-7133; (414) 255–4465.

CANADA

■ NEW BRUNSWICK
SAINT JOHN—JULY 16: Loyalist Days Doll Show by JPAM's Nun Doll Museum. 10 am–5 pm. 15 Jean St. E. Adm $2; seniors, $1.50; 4–12, $1. SASE to Pamela Trecartin-Cyr, Apt. #4, Somerset St., Building 1014, Saint John, NB E2K 2Y7, Canada; (506) 652–2894.

■ ONTARIO
MARMORA—AUG. 3: 13th Annual Show, Sale & Competition of Dolls, Bears, Miniatures & Supplies by Quinte-Hastings Doll Club. 10 am–4 pm. Marmora Curling Rink. SASE to Zella Reynolds, Box 204, Marmora, Ont., K0K 2M0, Canada; (613) 472–2819.

GANANOQUE—AUG. 9–18: Festival of the Islands Gananoque Museum First Annual Doll Show by Gananoque Museum and Lilacs and Lace Doll Club. 10 am–4 pm. Gananoque Museum, 10 King St. E., next to Town Hall. Adm $2. Lynette McLellan, curator, Gananoque Museum, (613) 382–4024; home, (613) 382–2082.

CAMBRIDGE—SEPT. 8: 15th Annual Doll & Teddy Bear Show & Sale by Maple Leaf Doll Club. 10 am–4:30 pm. Karl Homuth Arena, Hamilton St. Adm $3; children, $1. Judie Arnold, (519) 576–4238.

EVENTS

■ CALIFORNIA
SAN DIEGO—SEPT. 13 & 15: Dimensions in Dollmaking by Imitation of Life Construction Company. San Diego Convention Center, Harbor Dr. Part of San Diego Quilt Show. SASE to Imitation of Life Construction Company, PO Box 531, Poway, CA 92074-0531; San Diego Quilt Show, PO Box 12600, El Cajon, CA 92022-2600.

■ MARYLAND
GAITHERSBURG—SEPT. 16: Cataloged auction of fine quality antique & collectible dolls by McMasters Doll Auctions. Gaithersburg Hilton. Absentee & phone bids accepted. Send for free flier or order catalog, $30 to McMasters Doll Auctions, P.O. Box 1755, Cambridge, OH 43725; (800) 842–3526.

■ OHIO
CAMBRIDGE—JULY 13: Uncataloged Treasure Hunt Auction of antique, modern & collectible dolls. Pritchard-Laughlin Center, I-70, Exit 176. SASE to McMasters Doll Auctions, P.O. Box 1755, Cambridge, OH 43725; (800) 842–3526.

CAMBRIDGE—AUG. 3: Uncataloged Treasure Hunt Auction of antique, modern & collectible dolls. Pritchard-Laughlin Center, I-70, Exit 176. SASE to McMasters Doll Auctions, P.O. Box 1755, Cambridge, OH 43725; (800) 842–3526.

COLUMBUS—AUG. 16 & 17: McMasters Specialty Auction of Barbie® Doll & Related Items. Best Western Columbus East, I-70, Exit 110. SASE to McMasters Doll Auctions, P.O. Box 1755, Cambridge, OH 43725; (800) 842–3526.

■ OREGON
EUGENE—AUG. 23–25: 1996 Western Region Around the World Paper Doll Convention by Pacific Northwest Paper Doll Collectors. Salesroom, Sat., 1:30–4 pm. Hilton Hotel. Adm convention, $140; absentee, $85; salesroom, $3. SASE to Pacific Northwest Paper Doll collectors, c/o Kerlin Lisson, 1995 Monroe St., Eugene, OR 97405.

■ RHODE ISLAND
NEWPORT—JUNE 1–AUG. 31: 19th & 20th Century Christmas Decorations and Dolls by The Doll Museum. Mon. & Wed.–Sat., 11 am–5 pm; Sun., 12–5 pm. The Doll Museum, 520 Thames St.; Linda, (401) 849–0405.

Patterns, Parts & Pen Pals

Looking for Bajama Originals and out-of-print Kezi Works doll patterns. Will trade. Would like to correspond with women who make cloth dolls, especially dolls with adult figures and realistic faces. I'm 40 and an avid dollmaker.

Trisha Meigs, 124 W. Douglas, Canon City, CO 81212

Looking for original outfit and winding knob for 20" Thumbelina by Ideal. She was my most cherished doll as a child and I would like to restore her.

Josette Meese, 23302 Meadow Cross Ln., Katy, TX 77494

Looking for a dress pattern for my 18" 1890–1905 china shoulder-head doll. Doll lacks only a dress.

Norma Johnson, 1999 S. Packerton Rd. Winona Lake, IN 46590

Looking for right leg for an unmarked 19" vinyl/plastic musical doll. The leg is 9" long and about 5½" in diameter.

Myrna Nieves, 635A Little Britain Rd., #20, New Windsor, NY 12553

Desperately trying to find Disney Sleeping Beauty paper doll similar to one of my childhood (1959–1960s) and paper doll based on *Annie Oakley* TV series starring Gail Davis and Jimmy Hawkins. Looking for Kimberly and 1960s blond, long-haired Ruthie.

Barbara Elwell, 100 Seneca River Park, Waterloo, NY 13165-9729

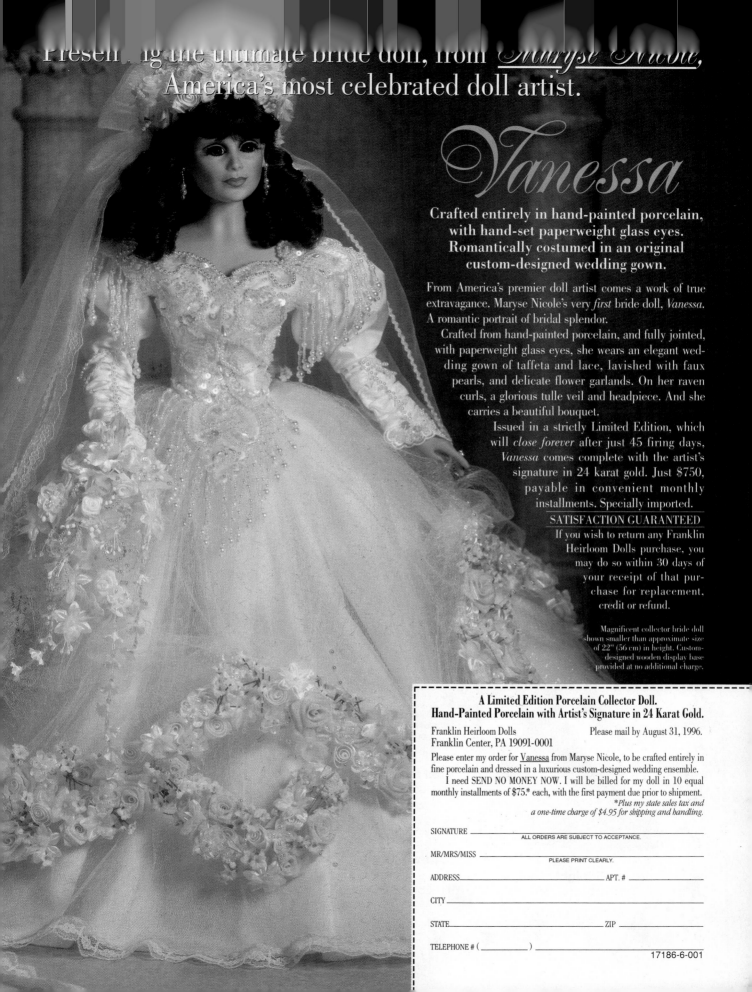

Presenting the ultimate bride doll, from *Maryse Nicole,*
America's most celebrated doll artist.

Vanessa

Crafted entirely in hand-painted porcelain, with hand-set paperweight glass eyes. Romantically costumed in an original custom-designed wedding gown.

From America's premier doll artist comes a work of true extravagance. Maryse Nicole's very *first* bride doll, *Vanessa.* A romantic portrait of bridal splendor.

Crafted from hand-painted porcelain, and fully jointed, with paperweight glass eyes, she wears an elegant wedding gown of taffeta and lace, lavished with faux pearls, and delicate flower garlands. On her raven curls, a glorious tulle veil and headpiece. And she carries a beautiful bouquet.

Issued in a strictly Limited Edition, which will *close forever* after just 45 firing days, *Vanessa* comes complete with the artist's signature in 24 karat gold. Just $750, payable in convenient monthly installments. Specially imported.

SATISFACTION GUARANTEED

If you wish to return any Franklin Heirloom Dolls purchase, you may do so within 30 days of your receipt of that purchase for replacement, credit or refund.

Magnificent collector bride doll shown smaller than approximate size of 22" (56 cm) in height. Custom-designed wooden display base provided at no additional charge.

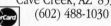

Classifieds

Here's the place to sell your products or to advertise for items wanted! Thousands of readers will see your ad! Rates are $1.50 per word with a $30 minimum. Be sure to send clear, legible copy (typewritten or printed is preferred) and include your name and address in the word count. For an acknowledgement, send an SASE with your insertion order.

Send check or money order to *Doll World*, Classified Advertising Department, 306 East Parr Road, Berne, IN 46711.

Deadline for the November/December 1996 issue is Aug. 1; deadline for the January/February 1997 issue is Oct. 1.

DOLLS FOR SALE

A DISCOUNT FOR you always! Spanos, Good-Krüger, Jeckle-Jensen, Goetz, Attic Babies, Happy Habits, Kish, Marlene Hur, Hamilton; teddy bears; more. Send 4 loose stamps to: Pam's Purrsonal Touch, 22 Garfield Ave., Medford, MA 02155.

FIND YOUR DOLL, paper doll or foreign costume doll on my list. Major companies. Full descriptions. Reasonably priced. Send LSASE: Carol Kindler, Box 12328, Philadelphia, PA 19119.

14 NEW PAGES popular dolls, clothes, lingerie, 1950s–'80s. $1.00 plus LSADSE: The Doll Trunk, Box 316DW, Hopewell, VA 23860.

DAWN DOLL IDENTIFICATION/price book—$21.45 (USA). Full color. Exclusive distributor. Buying anything Dawn, Upsy-downsy, Kiddle, '60s–'70s dolls, Christmas/toy catalogs. Joedi Johnson, P.O.B. 565, Billings, MT 59101; phone/fax (406) 248–4875.

ANTIQUE DOLLS: 17" Hertel & Schwab #151; 17" J.D.K. #211; 12" J.D.K. #260; 16" J.D.K. #260; 8" Kestner #143; 26" all-compo; 23" K & R #121 Toddler; Happy Holiday Barbies®, '89–'95; Bob Mackie and many more. Layaway is available. Call or fax: (402) 732–6705.

BIG DOLL LIST, $1.00, 2 stamps. Barbie®, Ideal, Vogue, Horsman, hard-plastic dolls. Winifred Freisinger, 4318 E. Des Moines, Mesa, AZ 85205.

BANSOO DOLLS©, SOFT-sculptured, very detailed handmade original designs by artist Brenda Sullivan. Dolls are 14 inches, signed/dated. Oliver Twist, Little Red Riding Hood, Jesus, Beauty's Vincent, Tobias (part Swedish, part African boy)—$79.00 each, two for $119.00. Brenda Sullivan, 2845 Windridge Drive, Apt. 11, Madison, IN 47250.

18-INCH CLOTH personalized doll, dressed as angel or in dress and hat—$40.00, pnpd. Sue Teichman, 1371 S. Aiken Rd., Owosso, MI 48867.

GORGEOUS 50TH ANNIVERSARY Barbie®—$1,500.00; Shirleys, Revlons, Kiddles, lots more; clothes. 12-pg. list, LSADSE. Don't miss these dolls. Dolls, P.O. Box 1805 (DW4196), Utica, NY 13503.

FREE LIST, SEND SASE and specify paper doll, modern doll or Barbie® list. Collector's Den, 895 25th Street, Batesville, AR 72501.

OLD AND MODERN compositions, hard plastics, rigid vinyls, Barbies®, personality, miscellaneous. LSASE for list. Gloria Faust, 4144 North Bridge, Memphis, TN 38118.

BARBIES®: EARLY BIRD specials on all 1996 new Barbie®! Also available. Dior, Goddess, Midnight Gala, Peppermint, Busy Gal and more! Layaway, mail/phone orders welcomed. Call: (905) 544–8196. Or, fax: (905) 547–1552.

MADAME ALEXANDER: NEW and recently retired. Friendly, fast mail order service. Newsletter, pictures, price lists. Send $2.00: Elegant Doll Shop-DW, 2848 Dog Branch Road, Prospect, TN 38477. Orders only: (800) 662–1232. Information: (615) 363–6680.

DOLL LIST! HARD plastic, composition, vinyl. Full descriptions. Separate paper doll list. Some Barbies® and accessories. Send LSASE to: Zaundra Rickson, 105 Brooklyn Rd., Pomfret Center, CT 06259.

THE ESTATE OF Darlene Mirijanian (Mirijanian Arts) including dolls of all sorts, old and newly created music boxes, toys of all types, Christmas novelties, miniature furniture, all are for sale due to her tragic passing. Inquiries are accepted by mail. Send to: Mirijanian, P.O. Box 734, Marlton, NJ 08053. All correspondence will be responded to immediately by telephone.

CHARMING 13" AWAKE/asleep cloth play dolls. Your choice of colors. My fabrics or yours. SASE for brochure. Emma's Charmin' Dolls, P.O. Box 14174, North Palm Beach, FL 33408.

WANTED TO BUY

WANTED! ANY ORIGINAL Wizard of Oz items: toys, games, posters, etc. Also, any photos of Judy Garland. Call Mr. Angelo at (315) 455–1165. Or, send info. to: 124 Royal Rd., Liverpool, NY 13088.

ALL LIDDLE KIDDLES, Storykins, Flatsys, Dolly Darlings, Upsy Downsys, Dawns, Rockflowers, Tiny Teens, Petal People, Finger Dings! Wanted for private collection! Have duplicates. SASE: Dawn Parrish, 9931 Gaynor Ave., Granada Hills, CA 91343-1604; (818) 894–8964.

WANTED! DESPERATELY NEED both arms for 1961 30" Miss Ideal, jointed wrists. Also, right arm for black Beatrice Wright Christina. Bernice Kulm, 916 Aurora St., Belle Fourche, SD 57717; (605) 892–3295.

PATTERNS & KITS

54 DIFFERENT DOLL kits, bisque finish. Pictures and price list, $1.00 (refundable on your first order). Elaine's, Rte. 1, Box 149, Hartland, MN 56042.

STILL #1: FASHIONS-to-Fit's unique pattern picture catalogs. Variety or Barbie® & Ken® & friends—$4.50 each catalog. P.O. Box 20A, Dows, IA 50071.

HISTORICAL FASHION DOLL patterns. Fits most 11½-inch fashion dolls. Send $3.00 for catalog: Lord Perry Historical Fashions, Dept. DW, 6041 Sanford Drive, San Jose, California 95123.

1920S BOUDOIR DOLL patterns. Brochure for stamped envelope. 32" doll and party clothes patterns—$9.90, postpaid. Catalog of decorative designs, people featured—$2.95. Sally Goodspeed, 2318 N. Charles St., Baltimore, Maryland 21218.

DOLL FACE PATTERN book for cloth dolls. 88 faces! Babies, clowns, children, adults—$10.00. Rathjen's, 1011 Benham, Richland, WA 99352.

FANCY PERIOD COSTUMES, bridal, wardrobe patterns. Barbie® plus larger dolls. Catalog, $3.00. Living Doll Fashions, Box 399, Alliance, NE 69301.

COPIES OF OLD commercial patterns for your childhood doll, mother's doll, grandmother's doll! Catalog, $3.00. Timeless Treasures, 4794 Norrisville Road, White Hall, MD 21161.

COSTUME PATTERN CATALOGS, $7.00. Barbie®, bridal, nationalities, historical, antiques. Doll/book list, $2.00. Married, moved! Joan Chiara-Cigler (DW), 7524 Lake Road East, Madison, Ohio 44057.

CROCHET PATTERNS. VICTORIAN elegance for 11½" fashion doll. Brochure, $1.00 (refundable on order). Mary Layfield's Creations, Rte. 1, Box 159A, Washington, WV 26181.

DUPLICATED COPIES OF outdated doll patterns. Send LSASE for list. Doll wardrobes, various sizes, available. Play Dolls, 539 Sargent, Jackson, CA 95642.

ANTIQUE REPLICA PATTERNS. Jointed bears, animal dolls, Golliwump. Very easy. Illustrated brochure, $2.00. Gaillorraines, P.O. Box 137, Tehachapi, CA 93581.

54 DIFFERENT DOLL kits, bisque finish. Pictures and price list, $1.00 (refundable on your first order). Elaine's, Rte. 1, Box 149, Hartland, MN 56042.

INDIAN DOLL PATTERNS, authentic costumes, 15": Sioux, Cherokee, Navahoe, Pueblo, Seminole, Iroquois—$5.00 each, $20.00 all. Free papoose pattern. Carolyn Mays, Martell, NE 68404.

REPRODUCTION CHINA HEAD doll kits, body pattern included. Look like old dolls, $1.00 for list (refundable with first order). Compo doll body list, $1.00 for antique and reproduction antique dolls. Carol Holy, 1732 Parkhill, Billings, MT 59102.

PROFESSIONALLY PAINTED PORCELAIN kits. Preset eyes, wig and body pattern. Your choice of eye and wig colors. LSASE for list and prices: Ruth Keifer, 2300 Shades Lane, Cumberland, Maryland 21502.

MINIATURES

DOLLHOUSE FURNITURE: 200 pieces to choose from! Send $1.00 for catalog to: C & K's Gift World, 4255 S. Buckley Rd., Dept. D128, Aurora, CO 80013. $5.00 off first order.

DOLLHOUSE! BEAUTIFUL, DETAILED, large, 2-story, fully decorated with hundreds of miniatures. Can send photo. $850.00 + shipping, OBO. (304) 876–1807.

FULL COLOR CATALOG on dollhouse furniture and accessories—$2.00 (refundable with first order). D.H.F., P.O. Box 23774-DW, Lexington, KY 40523-3774.

PAPER DOLLS

PAPER DOLLS, DOVER, Shackman, Queen Holden. Send $3.00 for catalog. Soldier Boy Miniatures, 3645 Upper Mountain Rd., Sanborn, NY 14132.

COMPLETE LINE OF Dover, Hobby House, Shackman and Texas Tech paper doll books. Also Peck-Aubry sets, magazine sheets, older paper dolls and archival envelopes. Price list/pictures, $1.00. Golden PaperDolls, Box 10697-DW, Golden, CO 80401-0600.

ACCESSORIES & PARTS

BARBIE® AND FAMILY clothes and dolls. New lists monthly from '60s to present. Send LSASE (3 loose stamps) or $1.00: Bendia Cushing, 310 Alexander, San Fernando, CA 91340.

DOLL EYES AND doll restoration. Write for free brochure on eyes for all purposes. Or, mail $1.00 for complete catalog on eyes plus all modeling, casting and filling materials for doll restoration. Van Dyke's, Dept. R13A9D6, Box 278, Woonsocket, SD 57385.

DOLL SUPPLY CATALOG: 66 beautiful wigs, shoes, stockings, clothing, crafter items—$2.00 (refundable with order). Simpson's Doll Supply, 6189 U.S. 68 North, Wilmington, OH 45177.

DOLL BLANKS, NO kiln needed, paint with translucent stain—$5.00, up. SASE for list. Marion Britton, Loma, MT 59460.

DOLL LABELS: ½-inch satin, up to 3 lines; ¼-inch satin, one line only. Standard SASE for sample card. 100/$5.00; 500/$23.00. Trudeau's Printing, R.D. 2, Box 35, Middlebury, VT 05753.

MISCELLANEOUS

"PLAY GOSPEL SONGS by Ear!" 10 lessons, $7.95. "Learn Gospel Music." Chording, runs, fills—$8.95. Both, $15.00. Davidsons, 6727DW Metcalf, Shawnee Mission, Kansas 66204.

NEED EXTRA MONEY to purchase those special dolls for your collection? Information on home parties, yard sales and wholesale business. Write: B.G.S., P.O. Box 23774-DW, Lexington, KY 40523-3774.

PERSONAL COMPUTER OWNERS can earn $1,000.00 to $5,000.00 monthly selling simple services part time. Get free list of 100 best services. Write: C.B.B.P.-HJ, P.O. Box 6035, Laramie, WY 82070.

Classifieds

Book & Catalog Reviews

African and Asian Costumed Dolls

By Polly and Pam Judd. Hobby House Press, 1 Corporate Dr., Grantsville, MD 21536; (800) 554–1447. Paperback; 6" x 9"; 176 pages; 250 photos; $14.95 plus $2 p&h.

This fascinating little book will please collectors of ethnic dolls and those who just want to read interesting tidbits about African and Asian nations. A short description of each country, often including history and culture, introduces the dolls.

The authors have included both traditional and current play dolls in their price guide. While no one can include all dolls from such a great number of countries, there is a substantial representation.

The Vivien Greene Dolls' House Collection

By Vivien Greene with Margaret Towner. The Overlook Press, 149 Wooster St., New York, NY 10012. Hardbound; 8¾" x 11"; 192 pages; 225 color photos; $60.

When this book arrived from the publisher, I immediately opened it to no particular page and became engulfed—with the photos, descriptions and details. "What a lovely book," I thought.

Later, I read the accompanying press release and discovered the author is indeed the wife of the writer Graham Greene, and there was another "Ahah!" in my head. I proceeded to really read the volume. I am as enchanted with the prose as with the photos. The mere mention of John Henry Newman, Sarah Siddons, Kenneth Clark and Dame Rose Macaulay only piqued my interest more. Here was an author whose work I could enjoy.

Do not be alarmed if these names escape you. If you are interested in dollhouses (our American term), antiques, history or life in the 18th and 19th centuries, you'll enjoy this book. It is a compendium of a life's work of saving old English dolls' houses, (for which Mrs. Greene deserves our lasting thanks). If you can't get to England to see this fabulous collection, buy the book and savor their uniqueness, beauty and charm.

A Century of Dolls: Treasures From the Golden Age of Doll Making

Photographs by Tom Kelley and text by Pamela Sherer. Courage Books, Running Press Book Publishers. Hardbound; 12" x 12"; 128 pages; 71 color photos; $19.98.

This book is unashamedly a "coffee table" book, and what a book it is! Tom Kelley's beautiful photographs enticed me to peruse the book, but Pamela Scherer's text kept me engrossed. Even though much of the material was familiar, I was soon off in doll land for an hour before I realized what had happened.

French and German antique dolls abound. The best bisque dolls are on display, but Googleys, characters and Alexanders are also included.

Sock Doll Workshop

By Cindy Crandall-Frazier. Lark Books, 50 College St., Asheville, NC 28801; (800) 284–3388. Hardbound; 7" x 10"; 112 pages; 50 black-and-white and color photos; 96 illustrations; $19.95.

Most of us have held or seen sock dolls. Those work-sock monkeys are probably most common, but if you think that's all there is to sock dolls, Ms. Crandall-Frazier will change your mind.

The directions, both general and specific, are very good, and I think the diagrams will help even the most inept seamstress complete these projects. Thirty projects using eight basic stitches are included. Best of all, they look like fun!

Traceable Faces for Cloth Dolls

By Barb Spencer. Jones Publishing, Book Orders, Dept. 10576, P.O. Box 5000, Iola, WI 54945; (800) 331–0038. Softbound; 8½" x 11"; 58 pages; $9.95 plus $2 p&h.

If painting and/or stitching faces on cloth dolls has been a challenge, you may find this book a great help. Several pages of instruction including selecting and preparing fabric and selecting supplies precede the pages of faces to trace and instructions for doing so. If you're anxious to start drawing your own faces but feel a little unsure, try this book. You should be painting faces with the best in a short time.

Creative Dollhouses from Kits

By Robert Schleicher. Chilton Book Company. Available in craft and hobby stores and bookstores. Softbound; 8" x 11"; 166 pages; black-and-white and color photos; $19.95.

Robert Schleicher has written a book for those of us who aren't ready to construct a dollhouse from the ground up and are confused by the dizzying selection of dollhouse kits on the market. In very straightforward prose, Mr. Schleicher explains scale, die-cut and saw-cut kits and trims before he gets to the specific directions of assembly.

After reading whole sections of this book, I feel confident I could purchase the kit requiring just the amount of work I wish to do and begin actual construction. Not content to leave you with the shell, directions and photos are included for finishing both the exterior and interior.

If you want to make a dollhouse from a kit, buy this book and keep it close at hand. I think it will save you some headaches and lead to a more enjoyable hobby.

Books, Paper Goods and Exclusive Gifts

By Theriault's, the Dollmasters, P.O. Box 2319, Annapolis MD 21404; (800) 966–3655.

You'll find books and auction catalogs covering dolls of all eras from Bru to Barbie®. Of equal interest to doll lovers are the desk top gifts, postcards, jigsaw puzzles and bookmarks. If you like to surround yourself with dolls, you're sure to find gift items for your friends—or yourself.

Bev Saxby

By Virginia Davis

Nursing and raising children have been set aside—creating dolls now has center stage.

painting colored glass slides for theater advertisements.

Marriage and raising a family became Bev's next priority. Now, since her children have grown, she can again concentrate on her art.

Teaching

Twice winner of the Robyn Hervey Australian Award, the New Zealand Gold Seal of Excellence and many other awards for her dolls in Australia, the United States and New Zealand, Bev conducts seminars in Australia and New Zealand when she can find the time. She has also taught in England where she demonstrated her sculpting techniques.

All dolls come in very small editions.

Bev Saxby

Bev's dolls' eyes are really the secret to their beauty and make her dolls distinguishable from those of any other artist. Since her specialty is eye painting, she likes to keep her eye secrets to herself, encouraging her protégés to develop their own skills. Her advice is to "be free, forget all the rules and just go for it."

The 1993 IDEX show in San Jose, Calif., set the stage for all the things to come. This was Bev's introduction to the American doll world and it was a tremendous success for her.

Bev's doll Lara was nominated for the 1994 DOTY awards. She says, "I love messing about in the various polymer clays." Her dolls are displaying more and more realism.

Bev says her dolls for the 1995 and 1996 Toy Fair will eclipse anything she has sculpted before. Perhaps if they become even more lifelike they will speak to us.

Many of Bev's collectors feel that her dolls are the most beautiful in the world. **DW**

Bev's dolls are represented in the United States by Judy Wallace, (800) 467–2354.

Australian artists have earned the reputation for realism and perfection in their dolls. Bev Saxby is no exception to that reputation.

The demand for Bev's work has strengthened her resolve to concentrate on truly amazing dolls in very small editions. Her desire is to make only one-of-a-kind dolls because her real passion goes into the original sculpture. Bev also thinks that the ingenious collector has become inebriated with so many limited-edition dolls that only real artistic ability will survive.

After her high-school days, Bev was awarded a scholarship at the Presbyterian Ladies College in Adelaide, South Australia. Her first job was

Jan McLean

By Virginia Davis

These dolls from across the sea are especially beautiful.

Below the equator lies a beautiful island in the South Pacific with a population less than that of New York City. This charming island known as New Zealand is the home of that extraordinary doll artist Jan McLean.

Only a few years ago, Jan would have never dreamed that she would be making dolls. She was very happy being a registered nurse in her home in Queens, New Zealand. The business of making dolls became so demanding that she gave up nursing.

Beginnings

Jan loved dolls and started making reproduction dolls a few years ago. Her grandmother had made papier-mâché dolls for her as a child. She enjoyed dressing the dolls, and she had a favorite doll from England that was a walking doll about the size of a 3-year-old child.

After making reproductions for a few years, Jan decided to make her own dolls. She used photographs of her children and other children and combined looks and expressions to create her own dolls' faces.

The results have been unbelievable. Jan's dolls have the quality and beauty of the antique dolls of the early 1800s. Every part of the doll and each article of clothing is handmade. Even the tiny jewelry and dainty slippers are completely handmade.

Jan says, "All of us at our little factory may work for a week on just one doll. That is why my dolls are so limited in number, because so much work goes into perfecting each doll. We assure our customers of the highest quality, and that is what they get."

Marigold's hair is made of mohair. Much of the clothing used on Jan's dolls is vintage clothing.

A Family Affair

Working with Jan are her daughter Kimberly and her sister Gaynai. Gaynai makes all the wigs for Jan's dolls from goat and surgical hair. Jan also says that Gaynai takes care of most of the business in their doll business while she pays attention to the design.

Jan's first doll was Calie, but by far her favorite doll is Marigold. She explains, "Marigold has such an independent spirit. She knows what she wants and goes after it. I think she is a little bit of a hussy, too."

The first of Jan's dolls which took the American market by storm was Pansy. Pansy is sold out and was modeled after Jan's daughter Kimberly.

Pansy is modeled after Jan's daughter Kim.

Doll Signings

It was quite an event when Jan signed her first doll. The doll was Pansy and Jan said, "I feel silly as a schoolgirl. This is lots of fun." That was in 1991 at Celia's, a doll shop in Hallendale, Fla. Jan still travels to Celia's doll shop for signing parties. Matilda is an exclusive doll made only for Celia's.

Primrose comes with three different wig colors and it could drive a collector mad trying to decide whether to purchase her as a blonde, brunette or redhead. Primrose's tiny angora sweaters are all handmade; each petite sweater cost Jan $200.

Jan is still in awe over her fame. She says, "I can't believe this is happening to me. I am so happy that the people in America and all over the world have accepted my dolls so well. It amazes me that so many orders came so quickly and there are more letters every day. I hope that I can make enough dolls in my lifetime so that all my collectors can have the one they want."

Jan makes dolls in editions of fewer than 100. She sells out her limited editions very quickly.

She will appear at signing parties in 1996. Her collectors can't wait to see what she has to surprise them with this year. **DW**